JUL   - 2023

Les Paul

70 YEARS

THE DEFINITIVE HISTORY OF ROCK'S GREATEST GUITAR

Published in 2023 by Welbeck

An Imprint of Welbeck Non-Fiction Limited,
part of Welbeck Publishing Group.
Based in London and Sydney.
www.welbeckpublishing.com

Associate Publisher: Joe Cottington
Design Manager: Russell Knowles

Original concept: Marçais & Marchand
Editorial direction: Nicolas Marçais
Design direction: Philippe Marchand
Graphic design: Thomas Hamel & emigreen
Design: emigreen
Illustration: Thierry Frieberg

A CIP catalogue record for this book is available from the
British Library

ISBN 978 1 80279 530 1

Printed by GPS, Slovenia

10 9 8 7 6 5 4 3 2 1

JULIEN BITOUN

Les Paul

70 YEARS

THE DEFINITIVE
HISTORY OF ROCK'S
GREATEST GUITAR

WELBECK

RICK BEATO

In 1912, my grandfather and great-grandfather came to the US from their home in Palermo, Italy. They went to work in the coal mines of Pennsylvania, sending money home to bring the rest of the family to the States. But when my grandfather got his first checks he ordered a guitar from the Gibson factory in Kalamazoo, Michigan. When it arrived… his father made him send it back.

My grandfather did eventually own Gibsons and I remember him playing them in the living room of my parents' house. And that story about having to send the first one back became part of my family's history. So when I asked my mom to help me buy my first electric guitar she was happy that I wanted a Gibson. My father worked on the railroad and my mother worked in the local can factory. There were seven children and we never had a lot, but my parents were incredibly supportive of our interest in music.

When I was 15 years old, too young to have a real job, I mowed the lawn of Tom Rizzo, the guy in town that owned the local music store. Mr. Rizzo asked around and found a used Les Paul Custom Black Beauty. I don't remember what we paid in the end but I remember when Tom said "$400" that my mom countered with a lower number.

Once I turned 16 I could get a job working in a grocery store. My friends laughed at my goal of saving one dollar a day so I could buy a white Les Paul Custom like the one Lindsay Buckingham played with Fleetwood Mac. I worked at the grocery store, ran track, played in a band and went to school. No wonder my grades were always pretty bad.

My mom chipped on that new white Custom and I gave the black guitar to my brother, John. I played that guitar into my early college years. As a jazz guitar major playing a Les Paul my college friends nicknamed me "Rocker", a name that stuck well into my forties. When I bought a 335, I gave the white guitar to my brother.

Then for a dozen years or more I didn't have a Les Paul, until my parents told me that for my 35th birthday they wanted to buy me a guitar. They told me to pick one out and they'd pay me for it. I found a black Les Paul Standard that carried me into my years playing in my first rock band. I bought a bright Fuschia Les Paul Classic as a back up.

Now, working on videos for the channel I have many guitars, but the majority of them are Les Pauls. Standards, Deluxes, Customs and Specials sit in a rack waiting to recreate the variety of classic recorded guitar tones. My Instagram feed is full of me playing them, almost vertically to fit in the frame. When I'm going to reach for an electric guitar to play something it's nearly always a Les Paul. I guess for all the reasons in my back story, they feel like home.

Rick Beato is the first online personality to get his own Les Paul signature model. Just like Les Paul himself, he is both a sound engineer / producer and a guitar player, well-versed in jazz and rock at the same time. His YouTube channel was created in 2015 and at the time of writing it has more than three million subscribers. His videos have been watched more than 500 million times, and he plays various Les Pauls in many of them. In 2021, Beato teased his upcoming signature model, a Pelham Blue double-cutaway Les Paul Special with two P90s, and the world is still waiting for its official release date.

CONTENT

8

The Man Who Invented Modern Music

26

Solid Gold

48

We Are Family

68

The Rise and Fall of the Les Paul

90

God Save the Les Paul

112

The Les Paul is Back

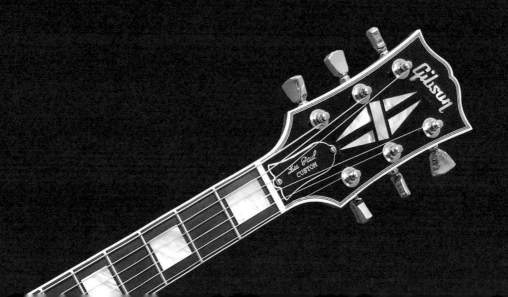

134
Big in the Seventies

160
Play Your Guitar on the MTV

178
Back With a Vengeance

202
A New Golden Age?

238
Index

The story of the Les Paul begins with the man behind the guitar. Just like everybody knows the saxophone without necessarily having heard of Adolphe Sax, most guitar players and rock music fans are familiar with the Les Paul but a lot of them aren't even aware of its status as a signature guitar. Back in the fifties, Gibson used Les Paul's fame to promote its new design, but during the seven decades that have followed, the tide has turned and the guitar has now guaranteed Lester Polfuss' immortality.

Lester was a typical American hero, a well-loved entertainer who had a vision and turned it into a reality. Or rather three visions: if not for his guitar model, Les Paul's name would still be noteworthy in the modern history of music for his work on early versions of the electric guitar as well as the invention of multitracking (also known as overdubbing or "sound on sound recording").

The tale of this true Renaissance man has been told many times, but as is often the case with such a legendary character, not all accounts agree on every detail. What makes it especially tricky to decipher the truth is Les Paul's own taste for hyperbole and tall tales. He would sometimes contradict himself from one interview to the other, and there is sometimes a fine line between boasting and telling about your past exploits in humorous undertones. He truly contained multitudes.

THE MAN WHO INVENTED MODERN MUSIC

LES PAUL IS THE FATHER OF IT ALL, MULTITRACKING AND EVERYTHING ELSE. IF IT HADN'T BEEN FOR HIM, THERE WOULDN'T HAVE BEEN ANYTHING.

Jimmy Page

Les Paul ™ EARLY LIFE

Lester William Polfuss was born in Waukesha, Wisconsin on June 9, 1915. Both his parents were of German descent. His father, George William Polsfuss (whose name had already been switched to Polfuss by the time Lester was born) was a farm owner who had also launched his car repair shop, while his mother, Evelyn Stutz, was a seamstress who would keep singing while taking care of the household.

Nick Lucas in the 1930s sporting his signature Gibson model.

She apparently wanted a daughter since the couple already had a son, Ralph, born in 1908, but she then became very supportive of the frail tiny redhead who became Les Paul. Lester had a knack for singing, dancing and entertaining – in the old-world sense of the term – back when "song and dance" was a career rather than a shortcut to fame and fortune. Back when he was only three years old, little Lester would sing for his friends, and at the age of seven he had already started tampering with his mother's pride and joy, the player piano in the living room. He had modified the melodies played by the pianola by punching new holes in the paper rolls, telling his mum "I'm making him better". At the time, player pianos were all the rage, since they allowed people to listen to music without having to play complicated pieces on their instrument. Sheet music was the main way for compositions to travel around before the gramophone and the radio took over, and the player piano was the first "background music" that didn't require to be played in order to be heard.

Clearly, Lester had a fascination for the process of creating music, and he seemed really into trying to understand the mechanical aspect of it. At the age of five, he had already been electrocuted three times after experimenting with the light switch.

He took up the harmonica at the age of eight, quickly became very proficient in it and started taking piano lessons. But he had heard the sound of a guitar on the radio, and it became an obsession. He got his first guitar, a Sears Troubadour, at the age of 10, and within three years, could already play it really well while singing along or playing the harmonica.

Les Paul was fourteen when the United States entered the Great Depression in 1929, and Wisconsin was one of the states which were deeply affected by the Dust Bowl, a series of dust storms in the mid-thirties caused by severe drought. The Polfuss family did not however lose everything, since they had already moved on from agriculture to fixing cars and driving taxis, but the context was not lost on Lester, who remained very conservative with his money for the rest of his life. Even though the guitar that bears his name would make him a true fortune, he would never buy anything new. He would

fix everything that could be fixed, and never bought a sports car or a fancy mansion. In fact, he bought his house in the New Jersey suburb of Mahwah in 1951 and lived there until his death in 2009.

As soon as he could perform a few songs, Lester – or rather Red Hot Red as per his early stage name, later Rhubarb Red – started playing outdoors, on local sidewalks and a drive-in restaurant. He was influenced by the guitar and banjo players he could hear on the radio (the Grand Ole Opry radio show had already started broadcasting in 1925), bluegrass artists and the "crooning troubadour" Nick Lucas, an early guitar hero who was the first artist with a Gibson model to his name. Lucas cemented the idea that Gibson was the choice of pros, the brand you could trust when you would hit the big time, which certainly imprinted on young Lester.

Lester Polfuss, aka "Rhubarb Red" in 1936 with his first Gibson L-5, a pre-1929 model with dot inlays.

EXPERIMENTING WITH ELECTRICITY

One of Les Paul's Logs. This one has a Gibson "script" logo and an imitation of the "split diamond" inlay typical of the Gibson Super 400 on the headstock, but the fretboard inlays betray the neck's Epiphone origin.

GIBSON
THE LOG

RICKENBACKER
"FRYING PAN"
LAP STEEL

The fact that the man who would give his name to the most popular signature model ever was deeply influenced by the first artists playing on Gibson signature models is a nice story in itself, but they had the same problem with their instrument at the time: volume. The Gibson Nick Lucas is a 12-fret small-body acoustic guitar with a flat top and mahogany back and sides, all elements that concur to a common goal, which is to get as loud as possible.

Back in the twenties, big bands were all the rage, and guitar players had a really hard time competing with blaring horns without the help of electricity. Freddie Green, who played in Count Basie's big band, was very skilled at using the archtop guitar as a purely rhythmic instrument, adding harmonic color by striking complex chords on every beat. Yet, not everyone was happy with that approach.

Many builders were trying to make their guitars louder using several mechanical tricks. The Larson Brothers, two Swedish luthiers working in Chicago, had invented a reinforced neck and top bracing that could support steel strings on an acoustic guitar. They had also created a massive guitar model with a huge jumbo shape, but it proved very impractical for players who weren't giants. Martin had tried the same trick with the dreadnought shape, invented in 1916 for the Ditson brand, but those bigger guitars would only produce a different tone while not being significantly louder. The Dopeyra brothers (hence the brand Dobro, who were operating under the name National at the time) developed the resonator guitar in 1926, putting a metallic cone like a speaker in the guitar's body, resulting in a bright, brash sound not unlike the banjo. The volume was there but the tone of the instrument did not match what jazz virtuosos had in mind. The Selmer Maccaferri model had an internal

LES PAUL

GIBSON
ES-150 1936

DROBO
HOUND DOG
DELUXE

resonating box on the 1932 guitars, but those would often come loose and cause buzzing inside of the instrument.

In the meantime, Les Paul had already started experimenting with electricity in order to make his guitar heard. In his early days, he would use a record needle plugged into a radio, a very crude version of a pickup into an amp. But soon, he got the intuition that amplification would be more efficient if the strings were the only vibrating part, not the top of the guitar. Therefore, he stole a railroad track, wired it to his mother's radio through a telephone receiver, and got exactly what he was looking for: power and sustain without feedback. At that point, his mother made a comment that would go a long way towards helping Les make history: "The day

GIBSON
NICK LUCAS KOA
ELITE 2015

that category, the famous ES-150 (ES for Electric Spanish, 150 for its price in dollars), a gorgeous archtop guitar with an understated look featuring Gibson's own design for a blade pickup, that would later be known as the "Charlie Christian model", nicknamed after the jazz genius (and friend of Les') whose two-year stint with Benny Goodman has changed jazz guitar soloing forever.

At that point, Les had become friendly with the brand Epiphone, whose factory was on 14th Street in Manhattan. He was allowed to use their facility on Sunday in order to work on his own projects, which is how he came up with The Log in 1941. This project started out with a simple 4x4 chunk of wood with pickups in it and an Epiphone neck attached. Les played that "broomstick with strings" at a show to a nonplussed audience. Remembering the wise words of his mother, he went back to the Epiphone factory and attached two sides from an archtop to his central plank, and the next show was a resounding hit.

"The whole experience taught me that the audience hears with its eyes. And not only was a stick of wood too difficult for me to play, but I looked like a geek. From that point on, it was obvious that any successful solidbody had to look like a guitar—no more ideas like building guitars from railroad tracks!"

Les built and used several "Logs" and he finally introduced the idea to Epiphone, who turned him down. Gibson didn't believe in the project either, and Les became known in the business as that crazy guy with the broomstick guitar. That didn't deter him from carrying on with his experiments, either on iterations of the Log or on so-called "clunker" Epiphones, archtop guitars that he would heavily modify to fit his needs, and that would usually end up with a large pickguard designed to hide the mess. Les Paul would even replace the Epiphone logo on some of those "klunkers" with a "proper" Gibson logo, since he already had become a Gibson artist before giving his name to one of their models.

you see a cowboy on a horse playing the guitar with a railroad track, you got a problem". At that point, Les understood that getting the sound he wanted was one thing, but he also had to capture his audience's imagination with how his instrument looked.

Those first experiments paved the way for a solid body guitar, and by the early thirties solid body electric lap-steels were becoming a reality with the Rickenbacker Frying Pan, developed with lap-steel player George Beauchamp, who had already worked with the Dopeyra brothers on the resonator guitar. During the thirties, a few brands got on the Electric Spanish guitar wagon by using magnetic pickups on traditional archtop instruments. In 1936, Gibson released the classiest and most enduring instrument in

FRIENDS IN HIGH PLACES

From a performing point of view, Les Paul's big break came very early in his life. He was only sixteen when he went to see Sunny Joe Wolverton, by then a Midwest star of sorts, perform at a local club. Word around town was that Joe would actually play above the third fret, which was a revelation to young Les. At the next gig, he brought his guitar along to try and borrow licks from the master, but the two of them became instant partners in crime as Sunny invited Les to play with him.

With the permission of his mother, Les left school and started playing gigs as the other half of the duo coined "Sunny Joe and Rhubarb Red". "Sunny" Joe was extremely influential on Les' playing: by then, Polfuss had only been playing for six years, so his style was not fully formed yet. Plus he was making fifteen dollars a night, which was a pretty hefty sum at the time (roughly the present-day equivalent of 250 dollars). Sunny Joe is also the one who took Les to the Gibson factory in Kalamazoo and bought him his first Gibson there, an archtop L-50.

The duo played their last gig at the Chicago World Fair in 1934, which is when Les Paul put together his first trio, moving from hillbilly music to jazz along with Ernie Newton on the double bass and Jimmy Atkins (Chet Atkins' older brother) on the rhythm guitar. The jazz trio format was not that popular yet, but the Les Paul Trio was the perfect vessel for Les to be heard without having to fight against a big band.

On a coin toss, they decided to move to New York (the other side would have been Chicago). The trio was struggling to get gigs, but Les kept trying to keep morale up by lying about his connections in the music business. He used to say "I know everybody", with the kind of confidence that can only come from a good liar. So the other two members called his bluff and asked him to call one of his connections in order to get more gigs. Les cold-called bandleader Paul Whiteman, got rejected, but still took his band to Whiteman's office (this was back when show-business people had offices where they could be reached). There, Les got escorted out by security in less than three minutes. In the lobby, they recognize bandleader Fred Waring who was waiting for the elevator. They started playing for him while the elevator was arriving, and by the time it was here they had been hired to join his band, the Pennsylvanians.

While playing with Waring, Les got one of the first Gibson ES-150s and started using that electric model, which caused a controversy among fans of the Pennsylvanians on whether this evolution was a good or a bad thing. Electricity won, and Les Paul was among the first jazz soloists to take advantage of that new sound.

In 1941, Les moved to California to form a new Les Paul Trio (actually a quarter with an extra piano player), and got hired to play background music for the NBC television company while trying to woo Bing Crosby, who was the ultimate entertainer of the day. During the war, Les got drafted as a musician and made records for the Armed Forces Radio Service record, and then finally got his trio hired by Crosby.

"Sunny" Joe Wolverton with his Gibson L-5 and Les "Rhubarb Red" Paul blowing his harp in 1935.

Les Paul plays for CBS Chicago in 1941 with a heavily modified natural Gibson L-5.

DJANGO UNPLUGGED

While Nick Lucas certainly left an early mark on Les Paul's playing, his style from the late forties and fifties owes a lot to his self-confessed biggest influence, Belgian genius Django Reinhardt. As early as 1934, with his band the Quintette du Hot Club De France, Django invented his own brand of jazz, called manouche, which used the guitar as the main melodic instrument (as well as Stéphane Grapelli's violin), a very bold choice at the time.

Les Paul's playing heavily borrows both from Django's driving rhythm style (nicknamed "la pompe", the pump, which drives and propels the whole band) and from his fluid and melodic lead approach.

It's also very probable that Les found the strength to get over his arm injury in 1948 by following Django's example, who turned his two missing fingers on the left hand (lost in a trailer fire) into an element of his style.

The two great men apparently met, probably back when Django was invited to play with Duke Ellington in New York in 1946. Les Paul was so surprised and humbled that his idol wanted to meet him that, when told at the end of a concert that Reinhardt wanted to see him, he replied: "Send down Jesus Christ and a pack of beer".

It is possible that Django heard Les Paul play the electric guitar during that concert, and that this concept remained at the back of his mind when he himself made the move to the electric guitar in 1951, resulting in his last and most beautiful recordings.

Django during his New York residency in 1946.

10 ALBUM COVERS
THAT MADE THE LES PAUL
EVEN MORE DESIRABLE

Throughout the years, the Les Paul has been a prized possession for many top-tier artists, which prompted some of them to wear it on their sleeve. Those albums, ranging from 1956 to 1998, showcase some gorgeous Les Pauls in the wild, and only one of them shows a Burst.

SISTER ROSETTA THARPE

Gospel Train (1956)

GUITAR: 1952 Gold Top Les Paul Model

Sister Rosetta Tharpe was a supremely important rock n' roll pioneer. She sang the gospel with a huge voice but her guitar playing was as gritty and wiry as anything Keith Richards would come up with ten years later. She has recorded a few songs several times over the course of her career, some of them on the acoustic and then on the electric with a band backing her. Gospel Train has Tharpe's gorgeous electric sound, and this is one of the few albums put together as such instead of the many posthumous compilations that have been released.

FREDDIE KING

Let's Hide Away and Dance Away with Freddy King (1961)

GUITAR: Gold Top wraparound Les Paul Model

This is the album that can be identified as patient zero, since Clapton wanted to emulate King's warm-yet-bright tone and the only clue he had was that cover. Since he couldn't find any Gold Top in England at the time, he had to make do with a Burst instead! And the rest is pure rock n' roll history.

THE ROLLING STONES

Get Yer Ya-Yas Out! (1970)

GUITAR: 1959 Les Paul Model Sunburst

This is the ultimate Rolling Stones live album. It was recorded in late 1969 in Baltimore and at Madison Square Garden, and is the perfect display of the powerful guitar interaction between Keith Richards and Mick Taylor. Their sounds perfectly complement each other, and they come from the guitars on the cover: a Burst, a Bigsby-equipped SG and a transparent Ampeg Dan Armstrong.

10 ALBUM COVERS

KISS

Alive! (1975)

GUITAR: Black Les Paul Deluxe modified with three humbuckers

Alive! started a thousand careers. American kids who grew up in the seventies all got turned on to rock n' roll by these weird-looking monsters in makeup and outfits on the cover of that album, rock stars straight out of a comic book. Even though the real live aspect of the performance has been highly debated, the three-pickup Les Paul in Ace Frehley's hands has become legend.

MICK RONSON

Play Don't Worry (1975)

GUITAR: 1968 Les Paul Custom stripped to a natural finish

Play Don't Worry is the second solo album released by Mick Ronson after his stint as part of the Spiders From Mars, the band that played with David Bowie during his Ziggy Stardust period. The glam rock master mostly plays cover songs from various artists (from the Velvet Underground to Pure Prairie League), and the cover is a pure rock n' roll pose with an outfit that has not necessarily aged well.

JEFF BECK

Blow by Blow (1975)

GUITAR: 1954 Les Paul Model modified with two humbuckers and an oxblood finish

Blow By Blow is the first "proper" Jeff Beck solo album, after a few outings with different iterations of the Jeff Beck Group. This time, Jeff is alone with his dark Les Paul, and this album is a fusion masterpiece produced by none other than George Martin. One year later, Beck had switched to a white Strat on the cover of *Wired*, which makes *Blow by Blow* even more precious.

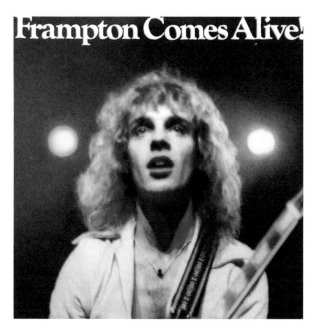

PETER FRAMPTON

Frampton Comes Alive! (1976)

GUITAR: 1954 Les Paul Custom modified with three humbuckers

This is it, probably the most important live album of a decade that defined and refined the fine art of the concert recording. This is a double album, featuring a 14-minute version of "Do You Feel Like We Do", yet it became a best-selling live album in the US. The cover only shows the unmistakable neck of Frampton's Custom, but the vinyl was a gatefold that would show the three-pickup body in its entirety.

THAT MADE THE LES PAUL EVEN MORE DESIRABLE

AL DI MEOLA

Elegant Gypsy (1977) / Kiss My Axe (1991)

GUITAR: 1971 Les Paul Custom (Elegant Gypsy)
1958 Les Paul Model painted black with DiMarzio pickups (Kiss My Axe)

Even though they were released fourteen years apart, these two covers share the same basic elements: Al Di Meola himself looking deep and moody, a scantily clad dark-haired lady, and a black Les Paul. On the groundbreaking fusion masterpiece *Elegant Gypsy*, that Les Paul is a Custom of the era, but on *Kiss My Axe*, it is a Burst that has been refinished in black.

SOCIAL DISTORTION

Somewhere Between Heaven and Hell (1992)

GUITAR: 1976 Les Paul Deluxe Gold Top

Somewhere Between Heaven and Hell is the fourth album by Social Distortion, yet this is the one that defined the definitive sound of the band, their best-selling record, and the definitive sound of an era. They could write and sing perfect pop tunes with a So-Cal punk flavor and a hint of country in their influences. The choice of a P90-equipped Deluxe Les Paul was the perfect instrument for that variety of sounds, and Mike Ness is pictured mid-jump with a guitar that became almost as famous as him.

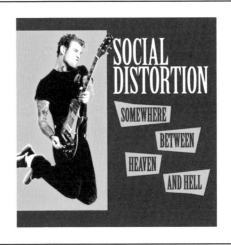

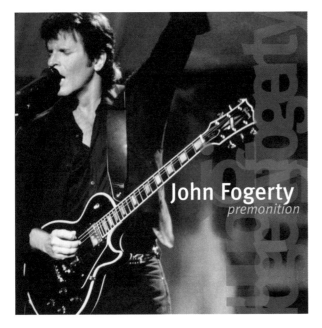

JOHN FOGERTY

Premonition (1998)

GUITAR: 1968 Les Paul Custom

Even though the band had broken up in 1972, John Fogerty was still known as "the former Creedence Clearwater Revival singer and guitarist" back in 1998. *Premonition* was his first solo live album, and the first time he decided to tackle those CCR songs that he had previously refused to cover on stage because of battles over publishing. With that album, he became the heritage artist that many wanted him to be, and he did it with the original CCR guitar, a 1968 reissue two-pickup Les Paul Custom, the Black Beauty on that album cover.

PLAYING BY HIMSELF

As a professional guitar player with a knowledge and understanding of audio engineering, Les Paul was feeling frustrated with the way he was being recorded. Bing Crosby suggested that he should build his own studio, which Les did, in the garage of his West Hollywood home on North Curson Avenue. Not only was Les Paul one of the first artists to create his home studio, but this is where he pioneered two techniques that are still at the roots of recorded music today: close-miking, as opposed to distant miking, which consists of putting the microphone close to the source in order to get every nuance of the performance, and multitracking.

Les had already been toying around with the idea of sound on sound recording for a while, but with that new studio he perfected the technique. Using two disc-cutting lathes, he would record a first part, then play on top of that part and record the two together, and so on until he got the sound he wanted. This meant that he had to have a very precise picture of the arrangements he was trying to get, since he was building from the ground up: given the sonic limitations of those discs, the first recorded part would gradually get buried in the mix, and the general result would lose a lot of high frequencies, low frequencies would lose their punch and noise would accumulate. He usually would start out with a percussive rhythm part, double or triple it, then move on to rhythm parts, then add solos, then finally add the lower guitar part that would simulate double bass, keeping that one for last to preserve the low frequency range.

He also developed a recording technique for his solos that would dazzle the listeners at the time: by recording his licks at half the speed, he would then sound incredibly fast and trebly when played back at the proper speed. This allowed him to get that signature speed-of-light-mandolin-sound, with some tape echo added for flash (another new technique at the time).

All this combined to create "The New Sound", the culmination of Les Paul's solo vision. He didn't need a band, an arranger or a producer, he could do all this alone in his garage. His first overdubbed songs, "Lover" and "Brazil", were released in early 1948 through Capitol Records. The California record company was the perfect

Several vintage ads for the Ampex Model 300.

fold for Les Paul, who had the support of a major partner to launch his radical vision into the stratosphere.

That opportunity was almost wasted later in 1948 when Les Paul and Colleen Summers, his mistress at the time, were in a car accident in Oklahoma. Les' right arm was so damaged that the doctors wanted to amputate it, but instead he convinced them to keep it stuck at the right angle to allow him to play the guitar. This new limitation only fueled his desire to push his sonic experimentations even further.

In 1949, Crosby, impressed by Les Paul's musical and technical talent, gifted him a reel-to-reel Ampex Model 300, which he quickly modified by adding an extra playback head to allow for sound-on-sound recordings. This happened at the right time for Les Paul, putting him at the top of his engineering game when he started recording with Summers, who was a country singer and guitarist. By then, they had gotten married and Les Paul had invented her even-more-American-than-apple-pie stage name, Mary Ford.

They started releasing hit singles in 1950 as Les Paul and Mary Ford with "Tennessee Waltz" and "Mockin' Bird Hill" in 1951, but really hit it big with their number one "How High The Moon". This single is an amazing showcase of what only two people can achieve with the help of a genius engineer. For this song, Les Paul has layered twelve tracks of guitars and Mary Ford's voice, harmonizing with herself. The four-part harmony right after Les' solo is particularly striking.

They released a few other hit songs after that, including "Tiger Rag" (1952) and the 1953 number one "Vaya Con Dios", all promoted by TV performances using Mary and Les' new tool: the Gibson Les Paul.

Mary Ford and Les Paul playing in their home studio in the early fifties. Les Paul is playing a clunker Epiphone, just before the creation of his Gibson model.

THE LES PAUL AND MARY FORD SHOW

In 1950, *The Les Paul Show* became a regular program on NBC Radio, featuring Les and Mary Ford interacting and playing together. In 1953, it became a short TV program on NBC Television, *Les Paul and Mary Ford At Home* (also known as *The Les Paul and Mary Ford Show*).

These five-minute episodes show Mary Ford and her husband chatting inside their home (usually the kitchen, the living-room or the garden), and playing two songs. They are the perfect image of fifties suburban life, complete with Mary as the perfect housewife and Les as the goofy husband who promises "not to eat crackers in bed".

The episodes were played five times a day, five days a week, and were sponsored by the mouthwash brand Listerine. Just like Les Paul did for his audio recordings, the 170 episodes of Les Paul and Mary Ford At Home were recorded at their home in Mahwah, self-produced so that they didn't have to pay for a professional soundstage and could still retain the rights to the program.

Back when black-and-white TV was in its infancy, this program turned Les and Mary into household names, and did a lot to promote the ubiquitous Gibson Les Paul.

Les Paul and Mary Ford in their Mahwah, New Jersey home in the mid-fifties. Les Paul is playing an early Les Paul Custom with one control replaced with an output jack, and the remaining three knobs replaced with chickenhead knobs.

PLAY LIST

NICK LUCAS
Tip-Toe Thru the Tulips With Me (1929)

THE BENNY GOODMAN SEXTET FEATURING CHARLIE CHRISTIAN ON GUITAR
Rose Room (1939)

BING CROSBY WITH LES PAUL AND HIS TRIO
It's Been a Long Long Time (1945)

LES PAUL
Lover (1948)

LES PAUL AND MARY FORD
How High the Moon (1951)

DJANGO
Nuages (1953)

LEO FENDER DIDN'T HAVE ANY CARVING MACHINES. THEY JOINED THEIR NECK WITH A PLATE IN THE BACK OF THE GUITAR. WE ALWAYS GLUED OUR NECK IN, MADE IT AN INTEGRAL PART.

Ted McCarty

SOLID GOLD

When the Gibson Les Paul Model finally came out in 1952, it was a revolutionary solid body from a brand that was not expected to go down that road, yet it also bore many of the points of reference that made it undeniably Gibson. The inventor and pioneer of the solid body Les Paul gave his name to that legendary instrument, therefore it would be logical to assume that he was an integral part in its creation. However, it has become clear over time that the Les Paul was not designed by one person, but rather by a group of like-minded individuals who came together to create a groundbreaking design.

PLANKS AND PADDLES

Gibson did not invent the solid body, and in that realm Les Paul is part of a club of tinkerers who turned that new way of approaching the guitar into a reality. A solid body is a purely electric instrument, a simple plank of wood that is not supposed to create a powerful sound when played unplugged, instead relying on magnetic pickups and an amplifier to do the job. The solid body was originally invented to create an amplified sound without feedback, which was the main problem with electric archtops as soon as a little volume entered the equation.

FENDER
TELECASTER '52
REISSUE

The concept of a solid body instrument had already been explored throughout the thirties and forties, especially with lap steels (Gibson had already made the solid body E-150 lap steel in 1935). There had also been a few early guitar experiments, notably by the brand Vivi-Tone, an historic name since its co-founder was none other than the luthier who designed the original L-5 archtop for Gibson, Lloyd Loar.

But the one solid body which paved the way forward was born in Downey, California on May 29, 1948. Paul A. Bigsby was a motorcycle racer and a foreman for a motorcycle company, used to welding metal and coming up with practical solutions for his customers. He started building musical instruments in his spare time in 1944, most notably multi-necked lap steels that were all the rage for the music genre that defined 1940s California: Western Swing, a mix of jazz swing, blues, hillbilly music and even polka. He designed and built his own pickups for those beautiful birdseye maple monsters, and he had already invented the pedal steel with the help of Speedy West when country guitar hero Merle Travis asked him for a solid body guitar. Travis

had noticed that lap steels sustained better than hollow body guitars, and he had an idea for a body shape that he submitted to Bigsby.

P.A. Bigsby got to work, and the result was a historic instrument that sparked a million fires, the first modern solid body electric guitar that worked perfectly and would become Merle Travis' tool of choice. The neck-through design would not catch on until Gibson's Firebird in 1963 (and it has since become a classic feature for heavy metal guitars), but the body shape bore more than a little resemblance to the single cutaway design of the Les Paul. The chambered birdseye maple body and solid birdseye maple neck gave it a charm of its own, and the pickguard that bore the name of its owner was typical country bling of the era.

Leo Fender was a good friend of Bigsby's, and that Travis guitar became the template for his experiments. The Fender brand was very young at the time (it was founded in 1946), and Leo was still looking for the innovation that would put his name on the map. His creation – which he started prototyping in 1949 – was a crude and more straightforward interpretation of the Bigsby guitar, featuring a bolt-on maple neck and a painted pine body. Fender finally came up with the Broadcaster solid body guitar in 1950, before it was renamed Telecaster one year later, since Gretsch already had a drum kit named Broadkaster. It is undeniable that he has been deeply influenced by Bigsby, so much so that his 1954 design for the Stratocaster headstock was unapologetically inspired by the Merle Travis guitar.

P.A. Bigsby was not interested in running a business. He made one instrument at a time and could barely fulfill all the orders he would get, and he didn't want to open a factory and change his process. So Fender did it instead. From the get-go, Leo's concept was a Fordian build philosophy to create a mass-produced, easily-serviceable instrument. Bigsby is mostly remembered today for his brilliant and beautiful vibrato design, but his legacy runs much deeper than that.

BIGSBY
MERLE TRAVIS
GUITAR 1948

Merle Travis with his Bigsby solid body.

Even though he's mostly known for the vibrato system that bears his name, P.A. Bigsby was a mechanic and a highly skilled luthier whose creations have greatly influenced bigger brands.

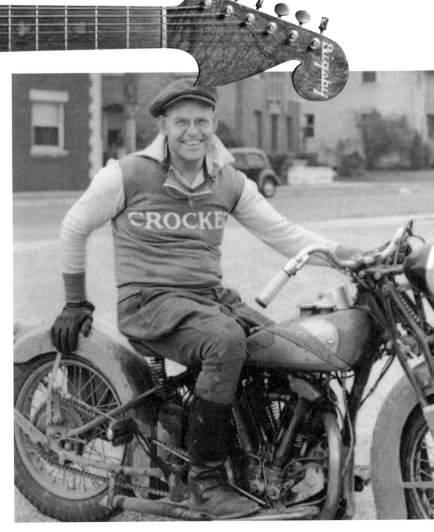

WHO MADE THE

Les Paul?™

Even though they had turned Les Paul down with his crazy broomstick guitars, Gibson eventually became interested in crafting their version of a solid body guitar in 1950. They wanted to give Fender a run for its money, while coming from a very different place: Fender was the new kid in town and could afford to throw paddles at the wall and see what would stick, whereas Gibson was a venerable company founded in 1902, and they had a reputation to live up to.

So when they started working on their version of a solid body, they took elements from their own catalog. Gibson president Ted McCarty was central to the process, but many others have contributed significant ideas and feedback, including salesman John Levy and guitar player Hilmer "Tiny" Timbrell.

A first prototype named The Ranger was a solid non-cutaway version of their hollow-body archtops, but it evolved towards a smaller body in the style of the ES-140, their diminutive ¾ version of the ES-175 archtop. A surviving 1951 prototype is extremely close to the look of the Travis guitar, complete with a sharp florentine cutaway and figured maple. The four-knobs-and-a-toggle switch control array (one Volume and one Tone control for each pickup) is the same as was already in place on the L-5CES, ES-350 and Super 400CES, and the definitive fretboard inlays for the 1952 production model were borrowed from the 1950 version of the ES-150 (whereas the 1951 prototype only had dot inlays).

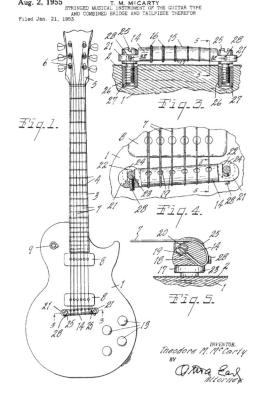

The prototype had a simpler flat top like Bigsby's, a one-piece maple top, less structurally stable than the two-piece they would end up with. Gibson decided to go for maple on top of mahogany for the perfect tonal balance: mahogany is warm and a little dark, whereas maple is bright and can be brittle. The mixture of the two enabled the perfect solid body sound, not too thin but not too muddy, with the perfect amount of sustain. The idea of mixing tonewoods on a solid body guitar was groundbreaking.

The patent for the Les Paul Model and its wraparound bridge, granted in 1955.

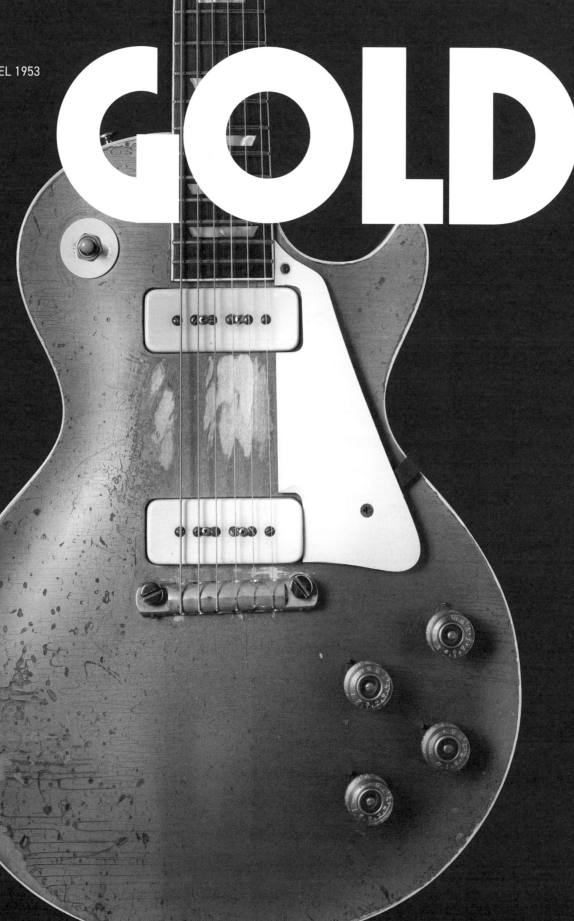

GOLD

RUSH

Gibson had a beautiful prototype for a solid body, and they needed to make sure the public would be aware of their daring new guitar. They had already designed two signature models before that, one for Nick Lucas and the other for the Wizard of the Strings, Roy Smeck. Both these models had been selling well, so they decided to go looking for a guitar player to spread the word around. It just so happened that they were already endorsing the most well-known guitarist of the day, and that guitarist had been toying with the concept of a solid body electric for decades, so he would probably be open to the idea of working with Gibson on this new model. Pairing with Les Paul was an obvious match, one that made sense from every point of view. Les Paul and Mary Ford had just released their first number one record, "How High The Moon", and that fame would help expose the Les Paul Model to many potential customers.

The historic deal took place in a hunting lodge up in the Pennsylvania mountains, where Ford and Paul were busy recording. They both tried the prototype and were impressed by it, so Les Paul agreed to a five-year contract with a five-percent royalty check.

But before the model was to be released to the public, it underwent a few more changes: Maurice Berlin, founder and president of Gibson's parent company Chicago Musical Instruments, was a violin collector and he came up with the idea of the arched top. This is probably the design element that defined the Les Paul, that made it the Gibson version of the solid body, a classier, more elaborate and more time-consuming build than the comparatively

rough Telecaster. Fender didn't have the tools to make an arched-top guitar. Gibson was the first historic brand to get into the solid body game, much to the chagrin of Fred Gretsch ("Ted, how could you do this? You know, now anybody with a bandsaw and a router can make a guitar."), but they definitely did it their way.

It had been said that the Les Paul was complete and ready to be built by the time the artist joined in, but from several accounts, it seems that Lester had three suggestions to make the guitar even better: first, he wanted a rounded cutaway, venetian instead of florentine, for the

This is the entry in the 1952 Gibson ledger for the very first Les Paul Model. It was shipped to a case company so they could take its measurements. Note the date: that historic instrument was the last guitar on a Friday.

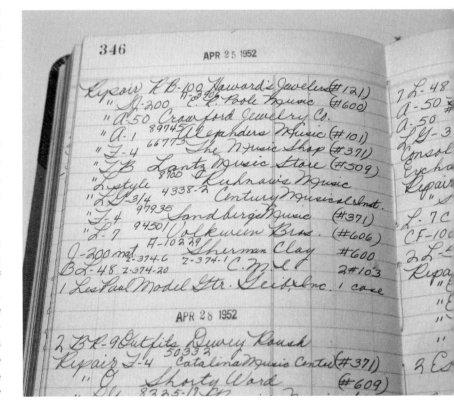

This early 53 model has the poker chip but it probably originally came with the trapeze bridge and was converted to a wraparound later. With age, the Gold Top finish tends to develop green spots that are really hard to emulate.

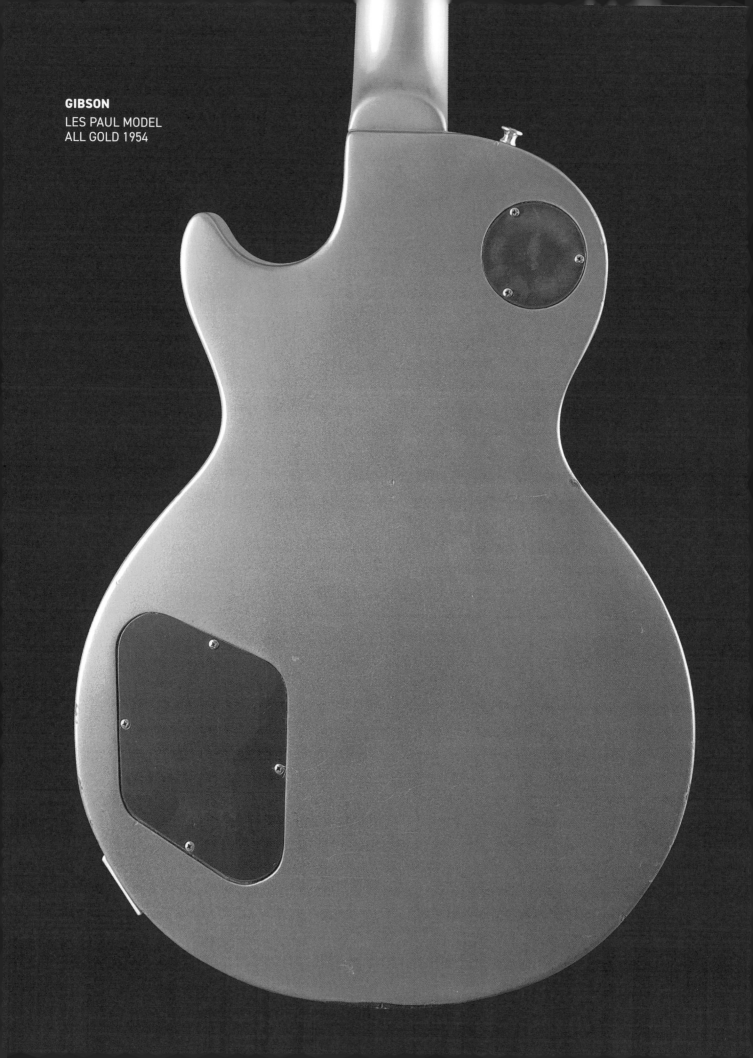

looks but also to avoid accidentally getting hurt while playing. Les also wanted to have a tailpiece of his own design on the guitar, which we'll get into later.

Finally, Les was also responsible for the gold color, which is a crucial defining point for the Les Paul Model, so much so that guitars from that era have been nicknamed "Gold Top" Les Pauls. Back in 1951, Les Paul and Mary Ford had performed at a hospital and one of the patients had asked Les Paul to get in touch with Gibson for a custom-order guitar. Just like they do nowadays with the Custom Shop, Gibson could build any guitar you wanted, and this man wanted an ES-175 (the laminate archtop jazz box with two P90 pickups) with a gold finish instead of the usual sunburst. The result was so gorgeous that even the Gibson employees were pretty excited by it, which is why it became part of the catalog in 1952. The ES-295 was an all-gold ES-175 with cream P90s and a floral pattern on the pickguard, and it became famous for being Scotty Moore's instrument of choice when he was playing with Elvis Presley back in 1954. It also featured the infamous Les Paul trapeze tailpiece, and most of its specs made it the bigger sister to the early Les Paul Model.

Contrary to the ES-295, the Les Paul Model was not all gold: only the maple top was painted, whereas the back of the body, neck and headstock showed the beautiful natural grain of the Honduras mahogany. Of course, as with all things Gibson, there were exceptions, and collectors lust over original "all gold" or "bullion gold" Les Pauls.

The gold finish on the Les Paul was a perfect way to hide any visual defects in the maple top, and it turns out that some owners who have stripped the gold finish from their old Les Paul have sometimes found three-piece maple tops or two-piece tops with an off-center seam. But it was also the ultimate flashy finish, a perfect way for Les Paul to quench his solid body sonic thirst while still performing with a stunningly beautiful instrument, and a perfect way for Gibson to make sure their brand new model would not go unnoticed.

Joe Bonamassa in 2014. He is holding an original 1952 Les Paul with no poker chip and the unmodified trapeze bridge.

GIBSON
LES PAUL
STANDARD GOLD
TOP

Some Gold Tops were "all gold" like the one opposite, but for most of them the back was showing the natural grain of the mahogany.

FROM DOG EARS TO SOAP BARS

GIBSON
ES-295 WITH
DOG-EAR P90S

Pickup-wise, the single-coil P90 was an obvious choice. Gibson's PU-90 (as it was officially called within the brand's nomenclature) had been their main model since it replaced the Charlie Christian in 1946. It was a whole different beast too, with individually adjustable pole pieces (even though the very early versions had hidden pole pieces) and a large black plastic cover with two extensions on the side that would earn it the nickname "dog-ear P90".

On the Les Paul, the pickups were mounted into the guitar's body, which allowed them to be adjusted in general height thanks to the two extra screws between the A/D and G/B strings. Without the extensions on the side, and with a new cream color to complement the Gold Top finish, these P90s have been called "soap bar P90s". The two pickups were placed far apart to get a maximum sonic difference, with the bass pickup being very close to the neck and the treble pickup extremely close to the bridge.

Gibson could have chosen to design a whole new pickup for their solid body model, since the P90 had mainly been used on archtop models beforehand, but it became a clear winner on the Les Paul, with a warmer and more mid-focused bark than the pickups Fender was building for the Telecaster. It might

not have been perfect for Les Paul himself, since he was looking for absolute clarity and the P90 is well-known for being slightly "hairy". To avoid that, Les Paul would modify his own model, leading to a new generation of clunker guitars, namely clunker Gold Tops with extended pickguards.

Nowadays, the P90 remains an extremely popular pickup on solid bodies for any style of popular music from jazz to heavy metal, and it can all be traced back to the original Les Paul Model.

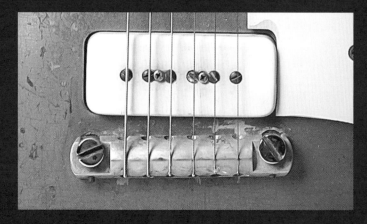

Soap-bar P90 from a
1953 Les Paul Model.

TAKE IT TO THE BRIDGE

Originally, the Les Paul was supposed to have the same basic trapeze tailpiece as the ES-175, the ES-350 and the L-5 of that era. This would probably have been a good idea, even though it owed more to the old world of archtops than to the brand new world of the Telecaster.

Instead, Les Paul insisted that his model should have a trapeze combined bridge and tailpiece of his own design, with a large trapeze tailpiece attached to a bar bridge. Ironically enough, Les himself would usually put Kauffman vibratos on his own guitars instead of using his own bridge. Clayton "Doc" Kauffman was an engineer whose name is mostly familiar since he was the other half of Leo Fender's first company, K&F (Kauffman and Fender) back in 1945. But before that he worked for Rickenbacker, where he designed the first vibrato unit for guitar, known as "Doc's Vibrola". Les Paul had bought a whole case of these and he would put them on most of his guitars, which makes it a true mystery as to why he chose not to have them on his Gibson model. Between that and the choice of P90 pickups, it is a possibility that Les wanted to release a solid body guitar that would correspond to most people's needs rather than his own. Maybe from the get-go his tinkering mind was racing and he was planning on modifying his own Gold Tops before even getting them. In fact, Les Paul's "number one" Gold Top, the first one he owned in 1952, was sold at auction in 2021, and it had been equipped with a Kauffman Vib-Rola and a neck pickup hand wound by none other than Les himself.

The trapeze bridge and tailpiece was designed by Les Paul to have the strings go over the top of the round metal bar. Instead of that,

Mary Ford and Les Paul during a press reception at the Savoy Hotel in London, 1952. Those brand new Les Paul Models have already been heavily modified. Both their guitars have a knob replaced by an output jack, a chickenhead knob and the neck P90 replaced by a DeArmond. Mary's has an ES-175-style tailpiece and Les' has a Kauffman vibrato. Note the third guitar on the right with its neck pickup removed.

GIBSON
LES PAUL
MODEL 1953

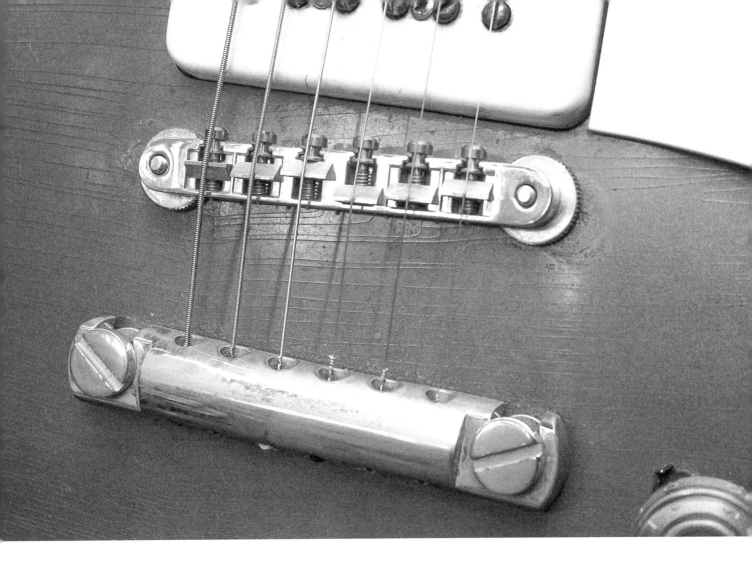

Gibson mounted them with the strings going under it, which would prevent players from being able to mute the strings in a comfortable position. Moreover, that bridge situation was clearly not working with the Les Paul Model's shallow neck angle, and the first Gold Top was off to a bad start because of that oversight. To this day, most vintage Les Pauls from 1952 and early '53 have to be modified in order to be played normally.

In 1953, Ted McCarty came up with the solution: a new combination bridge and tailpiece. This new piece of hardware was attached to the body with two stud screws, so it could only be used on solid body guitars. It could easily be adjusted in height, and had the right position for players who want to mute the strings. This new *wraparound* (or *stopbar* or *stud*) bridge, along with a new neck angle and the plastic cover around the toggle switch (the "poker chip"), solidified the first "perfect" version of the Les Paul Model.

Two ways of dealing with the unusable original trapeze bridge of an early Les Paul Model: a replacement trapeze designed by Nashville luthier Joe Glaser on an early 1953 model, or a sawed-off Tune-o-matic / stopbar combination to get them as close to the top as possible.

1953 Gibson ad featuring Mary Ford, Les Paul and two modified Gold Tops.

EARLY CONVERTS

HUBERT SUMLIN
WAKE UP CALL
1998

John Lee Hooker with an early Les Paul Model, complete with trapeze tailpiece and no poker chip.

Even though they were not perfect, those first Les Pauls were exciting new solid body guitars by a well-established brand. A few professional musicians took a chance on them and ended up liking what they heard.

Sister Rosetta Tharpe was a gospel singer and a scorching rock n' roll soloist, and she had already started experimenting with electric archtops as early as 1947 with an L-5. When the Les Paul came out, she knew exactly what to do with it, and the gritty sound of the P90s perfectly complemented her aggressive and highly energetic playing. She can be seen playing it on the cover of her 1956 album *Gospel Train*, and in 1957 this is the guitar she brought over to Europe for a U.K. tour. It checks all the visual boxes of a 1952 model with the trapeze tailpiece and no poker chip, and it is missing two of the four knobs (the "speed" knobs typical of the era) for the neck volume and the bridge tone. Those early knobs were prone to cracking, and the early cases were not great at preventing that.

The boogie man, John Lee Hooker himself, did a photoshoot in the fifties sporting a brand-new looking 1952 model. However, it is unclear whether the guitar belonged to him or if he had borrowed it to look dapper for the photo, or for how long he used it and what recordings he did with it.

Hubert Sumlin on the other hand used his wraparound model extensively (1953 or 1954). This Chicago blues genius had a thin wiry sound that he could get from any model (he also used a Rickenbacker and a Strat, which is really a case of the tone being in the hands), and he was the right-hand man for blues giant Howlin' Wolf from 1954 to the Wolf's death in 1976. The Gold Top was a gift from the singer to the guitarist, who used it to record the legendary riff for the 1956 single "Smokestack Lightnin'". Sumlin regularly appeared with his Les Paul for the rest of his life.

Howlin' Wolf's Chicago Blues rival, Muddy Waters, also used a Gold Top in the early fifties, before switching to a Telecaster.

Freddie King also started his career in Chicago, even though he was much younger than Muddy Waters and Howlin' Wolf, but he kept being rejected by the famous Chess label, which led him to try his luck elsewhere. He finally found a musical home with King Records in Cincinnati, Ohio - Freddie King on King Records, makes perfect sense. This is where he recorded his first session that produced his first two albums, *Sings* (1961) and *Let's Hide Away and Dance Away With Freddy King* (1962 - his name was still spelled with a Y at the time). He played a beautiful wraparound Gold Top on the cover of both those albums, which created a gorgeous electrifying sound on the instrumental single "Hideaway", a hit in the charts that borrowed from several blues pioneers. Several photos show that King's

JOHN LEE HOOKER

Exclusive
VEE JAY RECORDS, INC.
2129 SO. MICHIGAN AVENUE
CHICAGO 16, ILLINOIS

Freddie King and his Gold Top, minus two knobs.

Carl Perkins with his
Bigsby-equipped
Gold Top with no
pickguard in 1957
on the set of the movie
Jamboree.
From left to right:
Carl's younger brother
Clayton Perkins
on the upright bass,
Carl Perkins,
W.B. Holland on
the drums (he later
became Johnny Cash's
lifelong drummer)
and older brother
Jay Perkins on the
acoustic guitar.

Les Paul had the two Tone knobs missing, maybe two more casualties of a poor case.

The Gold Top was quite popular with early electric blues artists, and perhaps none of them had a more "modern" sound than Guitar Slim, a true blues guitar hero from New Orleans who released a series of magnificent singles from 1952 until his untimely death at the age of 32 in 1959. He was famous for dressing in an extravagant fashion and dying his hair in crazy colors, as well as a stage routine that would involve a very long cable to go play outside the club while his amplifier was still on stage. His main guitar was a trapeze Gold Top which he played through a distorted amp more than a decade before anybody else tried to explore those new sonic territories.

Finally, one last pioneer who put the Gold Top to good use was Carl Perkins, the rockabilly singer and guitar player who famously wrote "Blue Suede Shoes", "Honey Don't" and "Matchbox". Depending on the pictures or videos, he can be seen with either a trapeze model or a Bigsby-equipped poker-chip model with the pickguard removed. He moved on to very different kinds of guitars after that, but his immortal early work definitely bears the mark of those soap-bar P90s.

PLAY LIST

MERLE TRAVIS
Cannonball Rag (1954)

GUITAR SLIM
The Things That I Used To Do (1954)

SISTER ROSETTA THARPE
Didn't It Rain (1956)

HOWLIN' WOLF
Smokestack Lightnin' (1956)

CARL PERKINS
Blue Suede Shoes (1956)

FREDDIE KING
Hideaway (1961)

Sister Rosetta Tharpe playing her Gold Top in London, 1957.

> **YOU HAVE ALL KINDS OF PLAYERS OUT THERE THAT LIKE THIS AND LIKE THAT. CHEVROLET HAS A WHOLE BUNCH OF MODELS, FORD HAS A WHOLE BUNCH OF MODELS.**
>
> Ted McCarty

With almost 4,000 guitars shipped in its first two years of existence, the Les Paul Model was the proof that Gibson's foray into solid body territory could be a viable way forward for the company. At that point, the next logical step was to offer new Les Paul models in order to keep the customers interested. This is the start of a significant part of Gibson's modern DNA, which is the Les Paul range. Through the years, the Les Paul has had many extra words attached to its original name, from the Les Paul Professional to the Les Paul Gothic and so many others. It all started in 1954, when the notion of a range of models including a choice of various finishes was still in its infancy.

That year, Cadillac had the Eldorado convertible, the Series 60 Special, the Series 62 Sedan, the Series 62 Coupe de Ville and so on, and each model was available in about twenty different colors. The guitar business wasn't quite there yet: in 1954, most models were available in one or two colors, and every change in specs meant a brand new model instead of only changing part of the reference number. Fender's Esquire was a Telecaster without the neck pickup, and both were only available in butterscotch blonde. But in 1954, Gibson decided to expand the Les Paul line by creating two different visions inspired by their original solid body: the budget-oriented Junior and the luxurious Custom.

WE ARE FAMILY

GIBSON
LES PAUL CUSTOM 1955

ANY COLOR AS LONG AS IT'S BLACK:
THE CUSTOM

The Les Paul Custom was unapologetically introduced as the top of the Les Paul line on July 12, 1954 (for the Summer NAMM Show). At $325 (a hundred more than the Gold Top), it was a pricey proposition, proof that Gibson believed in solid bodies enough to offer them in a luxurious and classy package, just as they would for their beautiful archtops. The split diamond that graces its headstock is a telling symbol in itself, since it was only featured on their ultimate top of the line archtop, the Super 400, before that (that guitar was worth a whopping $550 at the time). Such an honour would have been hard to imagine two years prior.

As per Les Paul's request, the Custom was black – glossy black like a grand piano. Lester wanted a black instrument with a strikingly black fretboard (which was achieved by using ebony instead of the browner rosewood) so that the audience could see his hands flying around the neck. Plus black was like a tuxedo, which was the proper attire for a performer of the era. Mary Ford and Les Paul even requested two extra Customs in white in order to match their summer stage clothes.

Of course Ted McCarty was keen on the model for a whole different reason: "We added the Les Paul Custom just to have another one. (…) And there was a good reason for it. We were having more and more of a problem getting real good clear mahogany from Honduras. We'd get mahogany and it'd have streaks in it and whatnot."

Just like the dark edges of the sunburst finish could hide defects in an archtop's wood, black was the ideal way of hiding a visually sub-par piece of mahogany. In spite of the Gold finish, the Les Paul Model still showed mahogany in its natural beauty on the back of the body, so it had to look good. The Custom did not have that problem. Prior to that, black guitars had been rare custom-ordered oddities for Gibson, and no other model was available in that color by default.

That choice of color (which earned the Custom its nickname Black Beauty) could also have to do with Gretsch's new guitar. The Gretsch brand was established in 1883, which made it even more ancient than Gibson, and they had just launched their version of a solid body in 1953. The 6128 Duo Jet was semi-solid, with a chambered body that made it a hybrid of sorts, but it still represented the second serious solid body-ish offering from a well-respected brand at that time. Adding insult to injury, the single-cutaway arched-top shape was very close to a Les Paul, and the only available finish was… black. It wouldn't be too much of a stretch to imagine that Gibson's Custom was in part inspired by the urge to show those Brooklyn boys how it was done. Just like the Duo Jet, the Custom had massive white fretboard markers (including one at the first fret that wasn't there on the Gold Top), and the Gretsch Melita adjustable bridge may have pushed Gibson to use their own advanced design for a bridge.

But the Custom was a Gibson through and through, which meant a build quality that was second to none and an ornamental class of its own.

GRETSCH
G6128T GH DUO
JET SIGNATURE
GEORGE HARRISON

Tiny holes have been left in the top by a removed Bigsby, and the tuners have been replaced with those very classy Grover Imperials.

GIBSON
LES PAUL CUSTOM
1955

DON'T FRET

Gibson ad for the "Fretless Wonder" Custom.

Of course its black color wasn't the only thing that made the Custom extra special. Its very low frets made it very easy to play for the jazz virtuosos of the era, even though it has proven to be less than ideal for players who want to bend the strings, something that wasn't part of most musician's style back then. That special feature earned the Custom its other nickname of the era, the Fretless Wonder.

The Wonder also featured 24-carat gold-plated hardware, including the bridge, the tuners, the screws that kept the pickguard in place and even the pickup's pole pieces. Gibson had used gold hardware on some luxury arch-tops before, but its presence was not as striking on a sunburst or natural background. Gold on black defined the Custom's über-luxurious-but-still-classy look.

Multiple white bindings also surrounded each and every part of the Custom, from the top and back of the body to the neck and even the headstock. The headstock itself sported the aforementioned split diamond, but also a

bell-shaped truss-rod cover that said "Les Paul Custom". The Gold Top had the same cover without the name of the model on it, since that name was already written on the headstock. The Custom's split-diamond left no room on the headstock for that; therefore, Gibson found that smaller space for Les Paul's signature to remain present on the instrument.

Structurally, the Custom was very different from the Gold Top since its body was all-mahogany. The Custom did not feature a separate maple top, only mahogany that had been sculpted to give it that arched-top look. Paradoxically, that made the Custom easier to manufacture, as Ted McCarty would later explain with great cynicism: "So that Les Paul Custom was a solid body, it was not a sandwich, it was solid mahogany, but painted black. So you had some with streaks in it? You made Customs out of it. Dolled it up fancy with binding and other things on it, and sold it for a higher price."

The full-mahogany body made it slightly darker-sounding than the Gold Top, which was partly balanced by the brighter-sounding ebony fingerboard, but also a personality trait that was more in line with the warm round sound coveted by most jazz players of the era, who were the original target audience for the Custom. Interestingly, Les Paul himself thought the Custom should have been made with the maple top and the Gold Top should have been all-mahogany, but there may have been a communication mixup with Gibson.

CUSTOM HARDWARE

The pickup configuration is just as special as the rest of the guitar, and will forever be associated with the 1954 Custom, since it was only featured on the first three years of the model. The bridge pickup is a regular soap-bar P90 with a black cover and gold pole pieces, but the neck pickup is the rare Alnico V pickup, also named "staple" pickup for its longer pole pieces resembling six staples on the black cover. There had been a dog-ear version of the Alnico V that had previously appeared on a few high-end archtops (including the mighty L-5CES) starting in 1952, but this pickup remains famous for being the Custom's neck pickup. It was developed by Gibson's in-house pickup genius Seth Lover in order to compete with the clarity and openness of the DeArmond 200, also known as the Gretsch Dynasonic. The Alnico V was the last great single-coil design by Gibson, but it fell victim to the double-coil humbucker in 1957, which became the standard on almost every model at that point (but more on that later).

One last feature of the Les Paul Custom that was even more groundbreaking and important was its bridge. With the advent of the solid body guitar, players were becoming more demanding with the intonation of the instruments, since they could hear themselves more clearly and would often play way above the third fret, where a wraparound bridge could only reach a semi-satisfactory compromise. Enter the new Tune-O-Matic, designed by Ted McCarty who filed for a patent in 1952. This new bridge featured individually adjustable steel saddles that would allow the player to reach the perfect intonation for every string. What's more, that new bridge could be set up under tension, without having to loosen the strings, adjust the bridge, re-tune the strings, and keep going through those steps until you had it right. Vibration transmission was great, and the break-angle was perfect if you stringed it as it was intended, i.e. by wrapping the strings around the stop-bar. Many players have gotten into the

The Alnico V "staple" pickup.

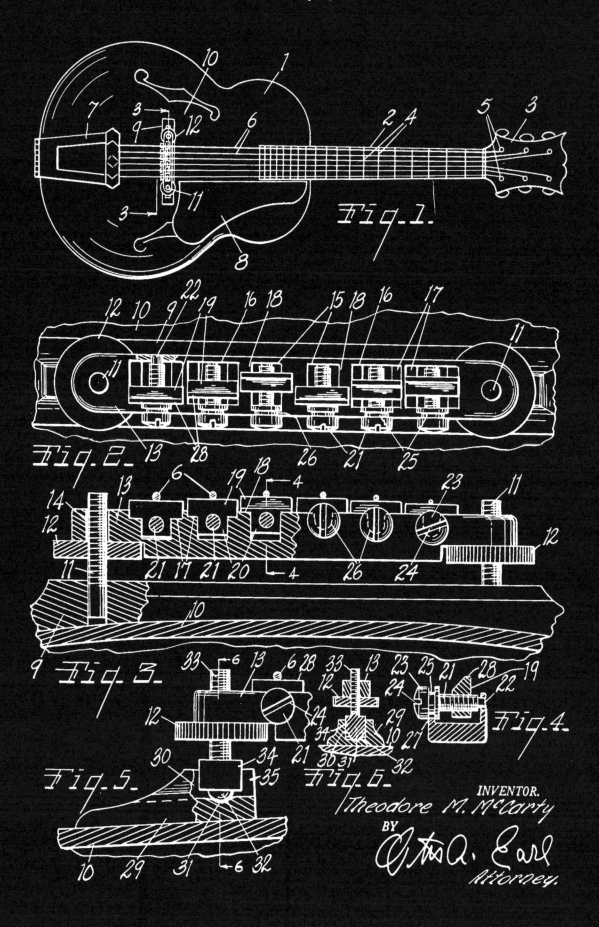

April 3, 1956   T. M. McCARTY   2,740,313
            BRIDGE FOR STRINGED MUSICAL INSTRUMENTS
                        Filed July 5, 1952

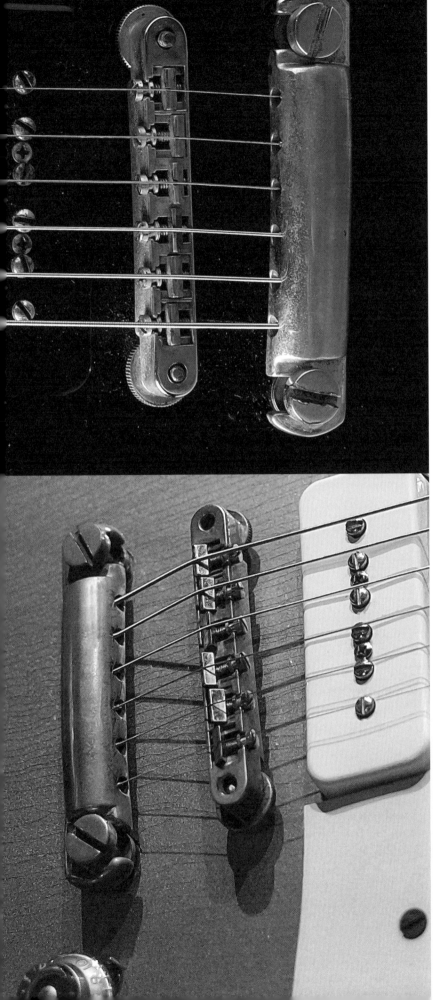

habit of only putting the strings through the stop-bar, which adds more tension on them, but recently a few top players have shown the "correct" way of stringing a Les Paul to the masses. The ABR-1 stop-bar was the ideal companion to the Tune-O-Matic, and the two of them remain the default choice for the majority of the Gibson catalog to this day. Using it on the Custom first was a way of showing how special and deluxe that new guitar was, but as early as 1955 the Tune-O-Matic started showing up on the regular Gold Top and became the new standard.

What's in a name? All the aforementioned features undoubtedly made the Custom a very special high-end guitar. Originally, Gibson was thinking of naming it Deluxe and it probably would've been a more appropriate name, since not much was customizable on the Custom: you had a choice of having it fit with a Bigsby vibrato, and that's the end of it. As such, the Custom is also the first Les Paul with a strange choice of name, a tradition that would continue with models like the Special, the Studio or the Deluxe, a name that ended up being used for a model cheaper than the Custom in the late sixties. Go figure...

1956 patent for the
Tune-o-Matic bridge.

The Tune-o-Matic
bridge on a 1955 Black
Beauty and a 1955
Gold Top.

CUSTOM-ERS

1956 Gibson ad featuring the Black Beauty and an earlier wraparound Gold Top.

The Custom was not a resounding success when it came out: in 1954, only 94 guitars were shipped, and 355 in 1955 (whereas 862 Gold Tops were sold that year). The jazz crowd who wanted costly high-end guitars were more likely to invest in a "proper" guitar (namely an archtop), and the more open-minded country and rockabilly players were more attracted to the fun-oriented and futuristic Fender models. Still, the very existence of the Les Paul Custom was a way for Gibson to showcase their exquisite craftsmanship, and also show the world how much they believed in a solid-body future.

Les Paul himself was the first in line to play that new model (and Mary Ford was obviously a close second), and he never looked back: even when the SG shape came along, he was using the Les Paul / SG Custom, and when Gibson made him his own Les Paul Personal model, they went with the Custom-style inlays. Once the Custom was released, Les Paul never played a Gold Top in public again.

Jazz-blues guitarist Mickey Baker was an early adopter of the model, which made perfect sense since he was a fan of Les Paul's. Les was the obvious inspiration behind Mickey Baker's project with Silvia Robinson, who also played a Les Paul à la Mary Ford. He was also a noted author of instruction books, including the 1955 classic *Mickey Baker's Complete Course in Jazz Guitar: A Modern Method In How-To-Play Jazz and Hot Guitar*.

Johnny Gray was another early Custom enthusiast, and Gibson made a special guitar

for him with three P90s (a Custom Custom!). He may not have been a household name, but he was an in-demand professional jazz player who played with Frank Sinatra and Nancy Wilson.

Franny Beecher was not a household name either, but he was part of a true revolution. In 1954, he joined Bill Haley's backing band, The Comets, just in time to start promoting the May release of "Rock Around The Clock". That song became a worldwide hit when it was used for the soundtrack of the 1955 film *Blackboard Jungle*, and it solidified rock n' roll as the sound of the fifties. Even though Danny Cedrone had played the blistering solo on the original recording

(he apparently used an ES-300), Fran Beecher is the one who appeared on stage and on TV performances of the song, playing a 1954 Les Paul Custom. This massive exposure has helped associate the Les Paul with rock n'roll, a pairing that would go a long way in later years.

During that era, the Custom also convinced another rock n' roll pioneer, maybe the greatest of them all. Even though he is not always thought of as a Les Paul player, Chuck Berry had a 1954-style Custom in his early days. He is usually pictured with a larger hollow-body ES-350TN, but his model is a 1956. In his later career, he became associated with the ES-345, but that model only came out in the late fifties. Therefore, it is very likely that we're hearing the Custom on Berry's groundbreaking debut single "Maybellene" in 1955, and probably on a few of the revolutionary singles he released after that.

Finally, one last artist that is worth mentioning is Marv Tarplin. Even though he

used a later version of the Les Paul Custom (namely a three-humbuckers post-'57 Custom), he remains one of the first and most influential pop musicians to have chosen the Black Beauty as his main instrument. Tarplin was the guitarist for Motown's first successful band, The Miracles (featuring Smokey Robinson). His playing on hits like "Shop Around" and "You've Really Got A Hold On Me" made a lot of budding players crave that sweet warm tone, all the more so since that Custom was very visible on the band's album covers, in 1961 for *Cookin' With The Miracles*, and even more so in 1963 with *The Fabulous Miracles*. That cover gave Custom envy to thousands of record-buying kids: the guitar is at the literal center of the picture, the rest of the band is dressed in gold but Marv Tarplin is the only one in a black tuxedo that perfectly matches his Les Paul. The stuff that guitar legends are made of.

THE **MIRACLES**
THE FABULOUS MIRACLES
1963

Bill Haley & The Comets in the 1956 movie *Don't Knock The Rock*, featuring Franny Beecher with an early Les Paul Custom.

GIBSON
LES PAUL JUNIOR 1956

THE HUMBLE

JUNIOR

The other variation on the Les Paul theme was the Les Paul Junior, the entry-level version of the signature model. This is one of those situations in which it seems fairly certain that the Gibson designers had a price in mind before they even started thinking about how they could make up a guitar model that would work with that price. And that price was $99.50, just sneaking in under $100!

Before the Junior, Gibson already had a tradition of building really good instruments at a fair price. They would make fairly-priced acoustics including the L-0 and the L-30 archtop, as well as cheaper electric archtops like the ES-125. They would even manufacture cheaper guitars under other brand names like Kalamazoo and Recording King. And just like the Les Paul Junior, all those instruments were admirably built and still fascinate musicians of today with their raw and warm appeal.

Usually, when Gibson built cost-effective instruments, they would skimp on the aesthetic side, keeping decoration to a minimum while still retaining a great build-quality with the same woods as the upper-tier models. And this is exactly what happened with the Les Paul Junior in 1954, at a time when the beginner's market was in dire need of serious solid body options to choose from. Silvertone had the quite inelegant 1375 model, built by the Chicago-based giant Harmony who had also launched the H44 in 1953. Funnily enough, the H44 had a small single-cut shape not unlike the Les Paul, and it was available in a copper color not unlike the Gold Top. It only had one neck pickup and sold for $67.50, and was of course built to much lower standards than Kalamazoo-made guitars. The

Esquire, which was Fender's cheapest solid body in 1954, was priced out of reach for beginners at $149.50. Not exactly a crowded market, and plenty of room for a new kid in town.

The Junior was basically a Gold Top with every single hint of sophistication shaved off. No maple top, just a solid mahogany body, no trapezoid inlays, just dots, no pearl-inlaid Gibson logo, just a stenciled one, no bindings anywhere, no fancy Gold Top finish, just a dark-to-yellow sunburst, and none of those show-off neck pickups, just the one you actually need. A beautiful flat-top piece of mahogany in the shape of a Les Paul, a mahogany neck with rosewood fretboard, one dog-ear P90 and a wraparound bridge. The pickup was so close to the bridge that it more than made up for the darker tone of the maple-less mahogany (it was moved a little further away from the bridge in 1956), and the whole thing gave a very mid-forward bark and immediacy to the tone of the Junior. Enough to drive any self-respecting jazz cat away, but an involuntary boon for rockers and punks fifteen years later.

The Junior was the perfect instrument to help beginners get better, as Les Paul himself said: "Finest quality instruments for its price, a moderate price. Encourage them to be a musician... instead of using a cheap instrument." It played easily, sounded great and looked the part too. Gibson was onto a winner as more and more people were trying their hands at the new solid body craze, and as early as 1955 the Junior largely outsold every other model that bore the Les Paul name. None of those buyers was a professional musician, but that part of the Junior's story would come in time.

SPECIAL SAUCE

Since the Junior was an instant success, Gibson was quick to offer different versions of that new best-seller. The first variation has become historic in its own right: it is the Les Paul TV, released in 1955. Even though it wasn't called Junior at the time, it was a Junior in all but name, except for its yellow finish, which justified the different name and the extra few bucks it cost. That yellow would largely vary from one guitar to the next (especially since they have all aged differently), and it is usually considered that the earlier ones are rather pale while later ones display a brighter yellow, sometimes nicknamed "banana yellow". That see-through finish was a nice way of showing the grain of the mahogany, and those TVs really have a charm of their own. In the official Gibson literature, the finish of the TV was called "natural", then "limed oak" (in reference to the limed oak furniture that was all the rage back then, even though the Junior was not made of oak at all), and finally "limed mahogany". Collectors know it by the name TV Yellow.

Conspiracy theories abound about where the name 'TV' came from: some say its color looked better on the black and white TVs of the era, others think it's a reference to Fender's yellow guitar, the Telecaster, but it more likely was an allusion to *The Les Paul & Mary Ford Show*, and to the fact that Gibson's premier artist was featured daily on the television. The Les Paul TV was a product "seen on TV", capitalizing on Les Paul's media presence by trying to convince watchers to buy their first guitar, which might as well be the one endorsed by that wacky inventor they hear and see every day.

1955 also saw the creation of the Les Paul Special. This upper-end model is basically a Les Paul TV with an extra P90 at the neck position (both pickups are black soap-bar versions on the Special) and a neck binding. But the Special was much pricier than the TV: in 1956, the list price of the Les Paul TV was $122.50, while the Special was sold for $169.50. Quite a huge difference for an extra pickup and neck binding.

The next model, released in 1956, was a three-quarter size version of the Junior aimed at children or players with particularly small hands.

Then, in 1958, the whole range was redesigned. The hardware remained the same P90/wraparound combination even though humbuckers and Tune-O-Matics had become de rigueur on the rest of the line, but the shape was changed to an almost symmetrical double-cutaway design with full easy access to the 22nd fret. With the transition to this very gracious but short-lived shape, the standard color became Cherry Red, a vibrant new hue that was much more revealing of the mahogany grain than the previous sunburst. The Junior, the Special and their respective ¾ versions were available in both Cherry Red and TV Yellow. That overhaul was a hit, and 1959 was the biggest year for the Junior, with total sales of 4,364 Cherry Red

GIBSON MUPHY LAB
LES PAUL TV '55 REISSUE

GIBSON
LES PAUL SPECIAL
TV 1957

GIBSON
LES PAUL SPECIAL
TV '60 REISSUE.

GIBSON MUPHY LAB
LES PAUL SPECIAL TV '55
REISSUE AND SG TV '61
REISSUE.

GIBSON
LES PAUL TV 3/4 1956.

Juniors, 543 TVs, 1,821 Specials and only 643 Standards (which by that time were finished in sunburst instead of Gold Top, but we'll get to that). That massive success may have been one of the factors that prompted Gibson to transition towards the SG shape.

Finally, the last variation on the "Les Paul goes cheap" theme was the cheapest one at the time, the Melody Maker. This 1959 model was actually called "Les Paul Melody Maker" in an early ad, but then Les Paul's name disappeared from the guitar. That cheaper model still had the single-cutaway shape with the darker sunburst of the early Juniors, but the pickup was a smaller lap-steel style single coil, and the narrow headstock gave it a look of its own. It was available as a regular of a ¾ version, both priced at $99.50, the original price of the Junior, which by then had been bumped up to $132.50.

GIBSON
LES PAUL JUNIOR 1958
CHERRY RED.

GIBSON
LES PAUL SPECIAL '60
REISSUE CHERRY RED.

Gibson INC.
KALAMAZOO, MICH
Made in U.S.A.

TREMOLO

DEPTH

VOLUME 2

FREQUENCY

VOLUME 1

MAX

MIN

MAX

MIN

HI

LO

MIN

VOICING

TREBLE

BASS

Les P

ON

OFF

70 WATTS

CYCLES

AMPED UP

The idea of a Les Paul line of products actually started way back in 1952, a few months after the Les Paul Model guitar was released. The players that were going to buy the new Gold Top solid body were also going to need an amplifier to plug them in, and Gibson would not let that amplifier be a Fender tweed. They came up with the Les Paul Model amplifier, also known as the GA-40, a gorgeous 40-watt combo featuring a twelve-inch Jensen speaker and a built-in tremolo designed by Seth Lover, three full years before tremolo would appear on a Fender amp. That first version was quite successful, culminating in 1,774 units shipped in 1953.

The GA-40 Les Paul Amp was revised in 1956 with a larger cabinet, a more efficient speaker and a brand new look, and then again in 1959 with a tweed-covered cabinet. The final version, released in 1962, had front-facing controls and a vinyl covering.

The Les Paul Junior also had a matching amp that started in 1954 called the Les Paul Junior GA-5 amp, a very simple 4-watt amp aimed at beginners. A rare Les Paul TV amp also became part of the line.

All those products are proof that Gibson thought that Les Paul's name had remained a strong selling point throughout the fifties, even though the relative lack of success of those models in the long run tends to prove the opposite.

This was also proof on Gibson's part that the solid body was here to stay, with a huge number of beginners learning their craft on the Junior who would hopefully end up buying higher-end models from Gibson as they would get better. To this day, no famous player has put the Les Paul Amp in the spotlight, which makes it a cheaper alternative than a lot of vintage Fender amps of the same era.

PLAY LIST

BILL HALEY
Rock Around The Clock
(1954)

CHUCK BERRY
Maybellene (1955)

**MICKEY BAKER AND
SILVIA ROBINSON**
Love Is Strange (1955)

THE MIRACLES
You've Really Got A Hold
On Me (1962)

YOU COULDN'T PULL BACK ON THE NECK, IT WASN'T STRONG ENOUGH

Les Paul on the SG model

THE RISE AND FALL OF THE LES PAUL

In the latter half of the fifties, the Les Paul was starting to sound like old news to the horde of young players looking for something fun, fresh and exciting. In order to keep it relevant, Gibson tried a few changes, some that would stick and others that would fail. In hindsight, most instruments from that era are seen as precious and highly valuable gems, but at the time they were the product of a well-respected brand trying to stay relevant.

MAKE IT A DOUBLE

GRETSCH
G6128T GH DUO
JET SIGNATURE
GEORGE HARRISON

Two versions of the three-humbucker Custom: a 1959 with a Tune-o-matic bridge and a 1958 with a Bigsby.

While nowadays the Gibson designs of the fifties and sixties are considered as "classics", it is important to remember that at the time they were as cutting edge as it gets. The company was driven by innovation, and several major manufacturers were fighting to get there first, to be the one with the new piece of hardware or design that would turn the market on its head.

Never one to rest on his laurels, Ted McCarty commissioned Seth Lover to design a new kind of pickup that would not be as prone to ground hum and buzzing as the P90.

A first prototype with dog-ear surrounds was built as early as 1955, and was perfected until it became standard on Gibson's high-end guitars in 1957. The humbucker, as it would become known (since it "bucked the hum"), was a double-coil pickup, two side-by-side coils with opposite polarities wired in series. The result: a sound unburdened by any electrical noise and, as a nice added bonus because of the two coils in series, a bigger, rounder and warmer tone than the single coils of the era. To help get rid of electrostatic interference, a "German silver" cover (made of copper, zinc and nickel) with a row of adjustable screws was designed, and thus the PAF was born.

The sticker on the bottom of an early 1960 PAF pickup.

Back then, the new pickup was just called "Gibson humbucking pickup", but it has been nicknamed "PAF" by vintage aficionados because of the sticker that Gibson would put on the bottom of the pickup that would read "Patent Applied For". The patent was finally granted in 1959, but the pickups still had the sticker until 1962, when it was changed to an actual patent number (which incidentally was the patent number for the Tune-O-Matic bridge, not the humbucker... confusing stuff). Either Gibson didn't want to display the patent number in order to stay ahead of the competition, or they still had lots of stickers in stock and wanted to use them.

Funnily enough, the competition was already getting there on its own. Chet Atkins was Gretsch's answer to Les Paul: he was a renowned guitar picker and a relentless tinkerer, and he had been a Gretsch artist since 1955 with two models to his name. Atkins was also annoyed at the hum from his Dynasonic pickups, and he asked the engineer Ray Butts (who had also designed an amp with built-in tape echo) to make a pickup that would eliminate the noise. Prototypes were tested as early as 1954, but Gretsch was a little behind when they released it on their guitars in the summer of 1957, a few months after Gibson's humbucker. The name was also a reflection of its function: since it filtered out electronic noise, it was called the Filter'Tron.

Originally, the humbucker was just a means to an end, a way of fixing the noise issue, but it turned into a different sound, a "bigger" sound that would quickly become Gibson's signature tone.

GIBSON
LES PAUL CUSTOM
WITH BIGSBY 1958

GIBSON
LES PAUL CUSTOM 1959

THE ECSTASY OF GOLD

The first guitar that received the new humbucking pickup was the ES-175, but it quickly spread across the range, even on higher-end models like the L-5 and Super 400. Only the cheaper models like the ES-125, the Junior, the TV or the Special kept on using the now-obsolete P90. But the ultimate guitar to display that innovation was the Les Paul Custom, which received three of them! Those three large pickups completely filled the space between the bridge and the neck for a stunning and intimidating look, and they were only controlled by a regular four-knobs-and-a-switch array of controls, and the middle position gave access to both the neck and middle pickup with reverse polarity for a quieter "out-of-phase" sound.

The 1958 Gibson ledger entry for the first two sunburst ("special finish") Les Pauls shipped on 28th May.

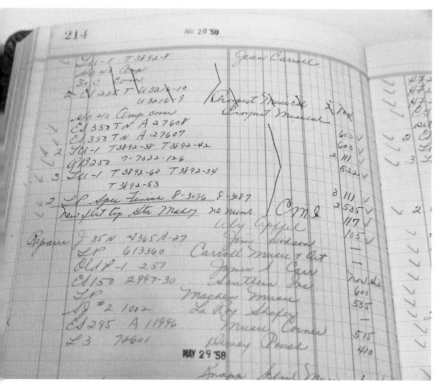

Of course, the Les Paul Model (or Gold Top) also became equipped with PAFs, which gave it the definitive look and sound that we now tend to associate with the Les Paul. The combination of the maple top on a mahogany body, a rosewood fingerboard on a mahogany set neck, a pair of humbuckers and the Tune-O-Matic bridge define a true standard, a set of ideal qualities that make perfect sense together and represent an achievement, the end of five years spent refining Les Paul's signature model. But in spite of that perfection attained, sales were dwindling down, and the Les Paul seemed to be out of touch with what players wanted at the time: only 598 Gold Tops were sold in 1957, so something needed to be done.

This is how the decision was made to change the color of the Les Paul in July of 1958. Since the humbucker had been introduced in the spring of '57, the PAF-equipped Gold Top had only existed for a little over a year. The new color was Cherry Sunburst. Sunburst was not new by any stretch of the imagination, in fact it was one of the older colors used by Gibson on early acoustics and archtops. But that new sunburst was Cherry, which meant it would go from dark red sides to an orangey yellow center. Gibson wanted something new, but not new enough that it would drive away its most conservative customers. The brand thought that the daring Gold color might have been responsible for the model's lack of lasting success, so they went back to the old ways – with a twist.

That new finish meant that the maple top was finally revealed. Therefore, woodworkers had to be more careful about how they would cut the maple, in order to have a two-piece top

These guitars were handmade, and sometimes weird things would happen, like the placement of the dot very far away from the "i" on the headstock of this 1958 Gold Top Les Paul.

with a proper center seam. The top was book-matched, which means that the piece of maple was cut in half and opened like a book in order to get a sense of imperfect symmetry in the wood patterns between the two halves of the top. That technique had already been used for the back of high-end archtops and for the maple-bodied acoustic J-200 (with stunning results on a natural finish), but with the Sunburst Les Paul Model it appeared for the first time on the front side of a guitar.

Obviously, not all tops were dramatically figured. Most of them were quite plain, and the best-looking pieces of maple would usually go to archtop backs. But some of them were absolutely spectacular, featuring varying degrees of flaming from light tight flames to wide tiger stripes. At the time, those figured tops were a fluke, not an option you could request from Gibson. Your Les Paul either had it or didn't, and that was it. Modern reissues of those late-fifties guitars have been made more predictable by choosing plain tops for the 1958-style models (which therefore are the less expensive of the bunch) and flamed tops for the 1959 and 1960 reissues. But at the time, it was much more random than that.

BURST INTO FLAME

GIBSON
LES PAUL MODEL
1959

Nowadays, that Sunburst version of the Les Paul Model is considered as the Holy Grail for guitar collectors and musicians alike. It is affectionately nicknamed "Burst" (for sunburst Les Paul) or Standard (a name that Gibson officially started using for the model in 1960), and it commands truly extravagant prices on the vintage market.

It was only built for three years from 1958 to 1960, and through those years only a few specs were changed: the frets became larger in 1959, the neck was made thinner in 1960, and

"reflector" knobs replaced the bell knobs during that last year of production. But overall, what makes those guitars truly special is not their objective specs, it is the minute variations that make them all unique.

The first element that can dramatically change from one Burst to the next is the color. At the time, they were all supposed to be finished in Cherry Sunburst, but even back then it could mean something different to different people. Some had a strong cherry color, others had darker edges (sometimes to cover imperfections of the wood), and the story goes that one of the sprayers at the Kalamazoo Gibson factory had decided he liked the darker sunburst of archtops

better than that crazy new Cherry Sunburst, so a few guitars bear his artistic sensibility.

Then, during 1960, Gibson changed the composition of its red dye, which usually resulted in a brighter red, almost orangey tint for the last Sunburst Les Pauls that got nicknamed "clownburst" or "tomato soup burst".

Since those original colors were applied by hand, they all vary slightly. But one factor has made them even more different from each other: time. Aging and exposition to sunlight has not been kind to the cherry hue, which has resulted in different degrees of fading of the red color in favor of the yellow, each nuance with a name: iced-tea burst, desert burst, honey burst, faded honey burst, tobacco burst, fire burst, bourbon burst, lemon burst or unburst (when only the yellow remains), dirty lemon burst...

Those names have been made-up by the collector's community, but they have also been used later on by Gibson themselves to classify their reissue Les Pauls. For vintage Bursts, the original color can easily be seen by looking under the poker chip, the pickup rings or the pickguard (if it has not been removed already), and fading can even create very specific patterns with random red spots depending on how the guitar was stored.

Another element that defines a Burst is its top. As previously explained, the tops are all different from one Burst to the next, and no two are exactly the same. Just like fingerprints, maple patterns are absolutely unique and they can help identify a guitar with a fair amount of certainty, even from a black-and-white photograph from the fifties, since fading does not

GIBSON
LES PAUL MODEL
1958 REFINISHED

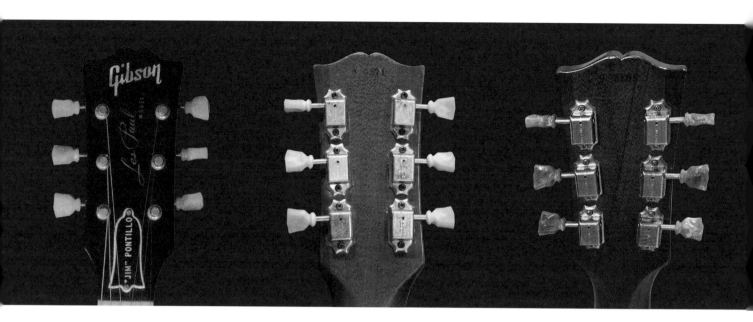

Back in 1959, a guitarist nicknamed Jim Pontillo asked for his name on the truss rod cover of his Les Paul, and Gibson was happy to oblige.

The first headstock shows modern replacement tuners, since vintage Klusons usually disintegrate over time, like the originals on the second headstock.

affect the flaming. Even the plainest of tops still has a defining element that makes it recognizable for the true connoisseur.

Since the necks were sanded by hand, they can also show small differences from one instrument to the next. But the last true element that defines a Burst is its pickups. It may seem strange since they were standard hardware parts, but PAFs are famous for having wildly varying specs. Depending on how they were wound, they can be brighter or darker, and their output level can make them sound hotter or thinner. And that's before taking aging into consideration, since corrosion by several factors (including the player's sweat) affects the way a pickup sounds. Also, they have varying colors hiding under the pickup covers. The coils are usually black, but starting in late 1958, they can also be cream (in which case they are called "double whites") or have one of each coil, which are known as "zebra" pickups. Of course since there are two pickups, one of them can be black and the other be a zebra, which makes for nine possible combinations.

Like snowflakes, original Sunburst Les Paul Models are all unique and quite easy to differentiate from one another for the trained eye (as opposed to Customs or Gold Tops for instance). At the time, that change was not enough for the model to regain the interest of the guitar-buying public, so Gibson stopped making them in late-1960. 434 Les Paul Models were shipped in 1958

(including some Gold Tops), 643 in 1959 and 635 in 1960. Among collectors, they are identified by their serial number (stamped on the back of the headstock) or by nicknames, which can be the name of a previous owner or a reference to the story of how the guitar was found.

That lack of popularity has caused their scarcity since few guitars have been built, which in turn has caused them to become extremely expensive after having been used by the best musicians of the next decades. Most of them have been accounted for and well-documented, but some of them are still out there, waiting to be found. Those "missing" Les Pauls have also resulted in fake guitars being sold to unsuspecting collectors for the same price as a real one, hence the joke: only 1,500 original Bursts have been made, and out of those 1,500 only 300 have survived.

Most guitarists could never afford an actual Burst, which has fueled the market for reissues and replicas. But it also fuels the dreams of many among us, who keep an eye out at yard sales, pawn shops and smaller music stores for that elusive Grail. Urban guitar legends abound of players that have bought a Burst from people who had no idea that they owned a true treasure and just wanted to get rid of their old guitar, and those stories keep happening often enough that the rest of us will keep on dreaming until we get our own "burst-under-the-bed" life-changing experience.

If the pickguard has not been removed before, it is a great way to see the original red color that used to be on the whole guitar before it faded away.

GIBSON
LES PAUL MODEL 1959

THAT OLD GUITAR IN THE CLOSET

The cable was used to plug into the family's stereo. The case and the straps were also part of the original treasure found in the Parisian suburbs.

It's just like winning the lottery: we've all heard the stories, and although most of us will never get to experience it, the stories are numerous enough that we can keep hoping and dreaming. Many original Bursts are still unaccounted for, and as the Baby Boomers are starting to vanish, we can expect some more of them to pop up under beds or in closets.

In May 2022, a lady was looking to insure a guitar purchased by her dad in 1967, so she brought it to a store that identified it as a 1960 Les Paul Standard with an added Bigsby vibrato. The guitar was in a barely-playable sorry state, but it was bought by none other than Joe Bonamassa, who was touring in England at the same time.

Less than a month later, another 1960 was found in a French closet. In the sixties, a Parisian tailor received the guitar as a trade for a job he had done, and he would sometimes play it in the living room by plugging it into the home stereo. But in 1968 the family moved to the suburbs, and Monsieur Victor had so much work to do that he couldn't find a minute to play his guitar, so he stored it in a closet.

54 years later, after the passing of his father, Monsieur Victor's son was cleaning his dad's house and he stumbled upon an old guitar case. He asked a player friend of his, who advised him to talk to Laurent Murelli, owner of the Guitare Village store in Domont. The verdict was almost instantaneous: 0 2185, or as it would become known "La Parisienne", is one of the absolute cleanest early 1960 Bursts to have ever surfaced. Early 1960 Les Pauls still had the aniline dye to create the red hue of the sunburst, and that would fade away really easily when exposed to sunlight, as opposed to the later shade of red that made up the "Tomato Soup Sunburst" of late

1960 Bursts. La Parisienne still has all its red, which is unheard of for a Burst of that era, and this can only happen by storing it away. This guitar is a true time capsule, since it has not been modified or altered in any way, and it shows us the true original color that most Les Pauls would come in back when they were brand new. The buyer of this incredible collector's treasure is none other than Slash, which is a worthy conclusion to a great story.

Next time you visit your elderly relatives, don't forget to take a look in the closet!

VICTIM OF CHANGES

GRETSCH
G6136TG WHITE FALCON

THE VENTURES
WALK DON'T RUN
1960

The commercial failure of the Les Paul Standard can be explained in many ways, the main reason being that the guitar market had drastically changed from when the guitar was first released in 1952. The musical tide was rapidly changing, and people like Les Paul were yesterday's news. Les Paul and Mary Ford's last top-ten single was released in 1955, and since then a new wave of entertainers had changed the music business landscape. Rumor has it that Gibson did not send a Sunburst version of the Les Paul to Lester himself, probably because he had found his ideal guitar with the Custom, but also maybe because they knew that seeing the new guitar in the hands of its namesake would probably not drive the sales up.

Elvis Presley took the world by storm in 1956, with a groundbreaking first LP and a memorable performance on TV for *The Milton Berle Show* (accompanied by Scotty Moore and his natural Gibson L-5 CESN with Alnico V pickups). In his wake, rockers redefined what a guitar should do, with groundbreaking singles like "Rebel Rouser" by Duane Eddy (1958), "Rumble" by Link Wray (1958) ,"Walk Don't Run" by The Ventures (1960) and "Let's Go Trippin'" by Dick Dale (1961).

Those players didn't pick on a Les Paul. Duane Eddy played a Gretsch, Link Wray had a cheap Supro and an even-cheaper Danelectro, The Ventures and Dick Dale had chosen Fender. Fender is the colorful elephant in the room when trying to understand the demise of the Les Paul: in 1954, the Stratocaster was invented and turned the solid body world on its head. By 1958, they had released the Jazzmaster and were starting to use automotive paint for fun custom colors. Even Gretsch, which was an older

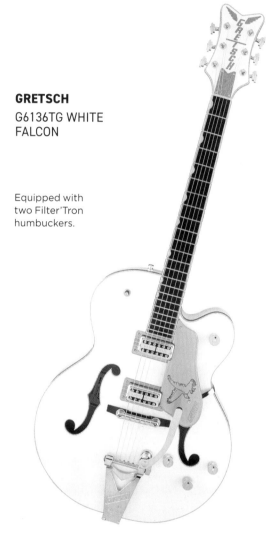

Equipped with two Filter'Tron humbuckers.

brand like Gibson, was more in tune with what the players wanted, with its cool car-inspired finishes (including Cadillac Green, Firebird Red and Silver Sparkle) and the ultimate bling guitar, the White Falcon, which had a kitsch charm very much of its time that the Les Paul Custom and the L-5 could only dream of.

It was not for lack of trying either: in 1958, Gibson released two strongly outlandish designs, the Explorer and the Flying V. These two were an overcorrection of sorts and they performed very poorly (even though, just like the Les Paul, time has turned them into Holy Grails in their own right). In 1960, Gibson was either too forward-thinking or too conservative, depending on the models.

I BOUGHT THAT IN 1959

Here are the prices of a few goods in 1959 and in 2022. For the guitars and car, the prices are an approximation of the amount you could currently get for a 1959 model.

	1959	2022	Increase %
Les Paul Junior double cut	$132.50	$12,000	9,050%
Les Paul Junior Three Quarter cherry double cut	$132.50	$5,000	3,775%
Special Cherry or Cream	$195	$12,000	6,150%
Les Paul Model (Standard burst)	$265	$300,000	113,200%
Les Paul Custom (black)	$395	$100,000	25,300%
Fender Stratocaster	$274.50	$35,000	12,750%
Fender Jazzmaster	$329	$20,000	6,080%
Cadillac Coupé DeVille	$5,252	$50,000	952%
Bottle of Coca Cola	$0.05	$1	2,000%
McDonald's Cheeseburger	$0.15	$1	667%

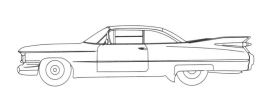

GIBSON SEES RED

GIBSON
LES PAUL
STANDARD 1961

This is the sideways vibrato with the arm folded.

The Les Paul was starting to look a bit dated, with a classic-looking design that didn't have the flash of the space-age Stratocaster. So Gibson decided to change it into a brand-new model: the Les Paul! The SG-shaped Les Paul, that is. In 1961 (late 1960, but who's counting), the Les Paul Standard kept the same name but everything else changed, and it transformed into the two-horned cherry-red rock'n'roll machine we now know as the SG.

The name SG (for Solid Guitar) first appeared in 1960 with the SG-TV, the new moniker for the TV Yellow double-cutaway Les Paul Junior. That change of model name, along with the Melody Maker without the Les Paul mention, were proof that Les Paul's name was not seen as an endorsement that would drive sales of the budget guitars.

All the reshaped Les Pauls would become SGs in 1963, allowing them to coexist with the "classic" Les Paul shape once it would finally be reintroduced. But for now, that new solid body is called a Les Paul, and it has a daring new look with a mission to make Gibson fun and current.

The new Les Paul Standard had very little to do with the Burst, apart from the humbucker pickups, the Tune-O-Matic bridge and the

parallelogram neck inlays. Actually, the new Les Paul owed more to the 1958 Junior, with its vibrant Cherry Red color showing the grain of a full-mahogany body (no maple there). Like the double-cut Junior, it had an almost symmetrical shape with two cutaways, with the upper one oh-so-slightly longer than the bottom one. And like the double-cut Junior, the new Standard had a neck that joined the body at the 22nd fret for an unparalleled access to the higher notes. That also turned the neck joint into a very fragile area, and many vintage guitars with that new shape have had repairs to the neck.

But the new Standard was a much sleeker affair, a mean guitar that felt extremely light and almost aerodynamic. The body was extremely thin, and made even thinner in places with the comfort contouring and sculpting on each side of the body, and inside the cutaways to make playability even better in the upper register. In fact, the body was so thin that the output jack had to be placed on the front of the guitar instead of the side. The cutaways were florentine (pointy) which, along with the red color, gave the guitar a "little devil with two horns" kind of look. That new body made for a surprisingly light guitar overall, with a sound that still remained dark and complex, albeit with a little less sustain and thickness overall than the old design. The new shape was the first Gibson contoured solid body, which allowed the player to hold it snugly against their ribcage like a Stratocaster, but it also had the perceived "longer" neck due to a different waist placement, like on a Jazzmaster. Overall, the playing feel was more modern and very different from the Les Paul of yesteryear.

The neck was surprisingly thin. Those early sixties necks have been nicknamed "slim taper" necks, and they are about as thin as it ever got for Gibson. Some players love them, some players have a hard time with them, it has become an acquired taste but at the time, this neck was groundbreakingly fast and easy to play. This thinness, along with the neck's placement clear out of the guitar's body, made it slightly movable, and to some players with a firm grip, it could produce an unwanted vibrato effect and produce slightly out-of-tune notes when grabbing the neck too hard.

The pickguard was quite small, and this time screwed directly into the body instead of being suspended as on the original Les Paul. The Les Paul / SG did not take its inspiration from archtops. It also had a second pickguard, a small piece of black plastic between the neck and the neck pickup.

The crown on the headstock was a surprise: that inlay, which has also been called "thistle" or "holly", could be found on most Standard models of the Gibson line, as a way of decorating headstocks that were not deemed worthy of

the split diamond Custom inlay, but still were better than lowly decal guitars. The crown can be found on SJ-200s as far back as the early forties, and it also appeared on the L-4, the L-7, the ES-5, the ES-350, the ES-175, the ES-295 and the ES-335. The fact that it made its appearance on the headstock of the new Les Paul was a strong symbol of Les Paul's diminishing influence: his name only appeared on the truss rod cover, where it didn't occupy too much space and could easily be removed. The previous shape was so closely associated with the man himself that those guitars were Les Pauls without the shadow of a doubt, but those new Les Pauls were somehow less strongly linked. It almost seems like the new Les Paul was already prepared to become the SG even before Lester decided not to renew his partnership with Gibson.

This is the first year of the SG, and the bridge is a Maestro vibrato.

GIBSON
LES PAUL '61 REISSUE

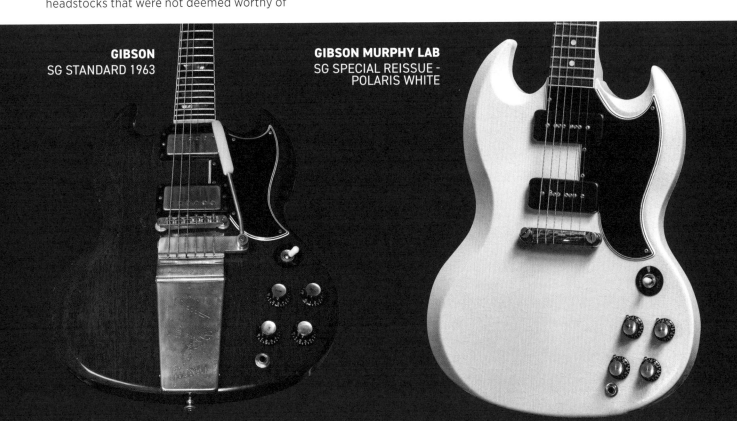

GIBSON
SG STANDARD 1963

GIBSON MURPHY LAB
SG SPECIAL REISSUE -
POLARIS WHITE

OVER, UNDER, SIDEWAYS, DOWN

Once the SG-shaped Les Paul was introduced in late 1960, the rest of the Les Paul line followed suit with a range of new guitars featuring that exciting double-horned new shape. The Custom remained at the top of the line, and it still had the gold hardware, the three humbuckers, the big block inlays and the split diamond on its headstock. There were bindings on the headstock and the neck, but the thinner contoured body prevented it from having the double binding of the original Les Paul's body.

The small pickguard between the neck and the rhythm pickup had the same "Les Paul Custom" logo as the truss-rod cover, and from late 1963-on, it just said "Custom". Instead of the Kluson tuners of the Standard, the Custom had heavier metallic Grovers, which tended to make them neck-heavy when playing standing up.

But the biggest and most obvious change on this new Custom was its color, a stunning white finish that looked supremely bling with the gold hardware. In a complete twist from what used to be the Black Beauty, the Custom was now light-cream with white pickguards and black pickup rings.

The new Les Paul Junior had the exact same shape as the other SG / Les Pauls of the era, with the same specs as the previous version of the Junior: single P90, wraparound bridge, larger pickguard, no bindings, dot inlays and stenciled logos. Interestingly, that was the only model of the new line that still had the bigger Les Paul logo on the headstock.

The Special wasn't even called a Les Paul anymore, it was already the SG Special and it had a neck binding as well as an extra neck pickup.

The Special and the Junior were available in Cherry Red and Polaris White (a "whiter" white than the Custom's light cream), and a few SG TVs were built but they remain a rarity. A few Standards and Juniors have also been made in gorgeous Pelham Blue.

Finally, the new Les Paul's modernity also came from its vibratos. The Standard and the Custom originally came equipped with the infamous "sideways vibrato", a big block of metal activated by an arm that could be folded in two that produced the vibrato effect by being pushed sideways (hence the name) instead of towards the body. That failed experiment would go out of tune all the time and most players chose not to use it at all, but the beauty of that unit still makes them desirable for vintage collectors.

In 1962, it was replaced by the Maestro vibrato, officially named the "Gibson Vibrola". Originally, it had an inlaid ebony block below the vibrato which has become a clear sign of a 1962 Les Paul, and then the big metal cover engraved with a lyre and the Gibson logo became standard.

The SG and Junior were available with a short Vibrola, a crude metallic contraption that could still yield good results when set up properly. Quite often, these have been replaced with more stable wraparounds on vintage guitars.

The "Les Paul Custom" logo between the neck pickup and the neck.

GIBSON
LES PAUL CUSTOM
1961

This is the sideways vibrato with the arm unfolded.

THE END OF AN ERA

Sister Rosetta Tharpe sings in the UK in 1964 with her beautiful sideways-vibrato Les Paul Custom.

Judging by the number of units shipped, it seems like the SG shape was the shot in the arm that the Les Paul needed to become relevant again: 1662 Standards were shipped in 1961 against 635 Burst Standards in 1960. That success would prove to be lasting, and sales were not impacted at all when Les Paul's name disappeared from the headstocks in 1963.

It has often been said that Les Paul parted ways with Gibson because he was not happy with the SG's radical shape, and didn't want his name associated with such a revolutionary instrument. However, Les Paul and Mary Ford appeared with matching Custom SG-shaped Les Pauls for ads, and they even played modded guitars with bigger pickguards (one black, one

clear) to hide the modifications and the hole left by the removal of the middle pickup, Clunker SGs if you will. Les Paul even went the extra mile to borrow a Standard SG-shaped Les Paul from a local shop so he could pose with it on the cover of the 1962 album *Bouquet Of Roses* (featuring a crooked smile by Mary Ford that can only be seen as a sign of their marriage unraveling).

But on the other hand, if he had to get a new Les Paul from a local shop for a photo shoot, it means Les Paul didn't travel with one, and this is because he would still play the older shape when he performed and recorded. In recent years, Tom Doyle, Les Paul's longtime guitar tech and friend, revealed that Les had a problem with the way the neck moved slightly ("He had a lot of strength in his hands. And with an SG you can actually create vibrato with the neck moving back and forth") and with the new sound created by that new design ("You just couldn't get the same kind of sound, resonance-wise because it was not the thickness of a Les Paul body and also it didn't have a maple cap on it like his Goldtop.").

Overall, Les Paul wasn't a fan of the SG shape, but he was a realist. He understood that this was the way forward, that most people wanted a lighter guitar with a vibrato, and that Gibson wanted a guitar that was cheaper to build. He did not renew his five-year contract for a third time in 1963 only because his marriage with Mary Ford was coming to an end, and he didn't want to share his royalties with the divorce lawyers. This is the simpler and much sadder truth to how Les Paul ended his relationship with Gibson, marking the beginning of a very dark period for the former star. Les Paul stopped performing and recording altogether during a five-year period

LES PAUL *AND* MARY FORD

BOUQUET OF ROSES

1962

Gibson ad for the new Les Paul Custom. This shows a version without the second smaller pickguard between the neck pickup and the neck.

from 1963 to 1968, and even after returning to the stage, he never really got over losing Mary. He never remarried and even though he had a few relationships, mostly lived a humdrum solitary life, fighting off depression by keeping himself busy all the time, repairing objects around his New Jersey house (the same house he had bought with Mary Ford that he kept for all his life) or modifying guitars in his kitchen.

Gibson's fate meanwhile looked radiant in the early sixties. In February of 1964, the Beatles' appearance on *The Ed Sullivan Show* started a national guitar craze, causing millions of young Americans to form a band overnight. The whole guitar market exploded, and manufacturers even had a hard time keeping up with demand. The evolution of the number of SG Junior models (priced at $155) shipped over that period of time is very telling: 2,318 in 1963, then 3,364 in 1964 and 3,570 in 1965. Similarly, the SG Special in Cherry Red went from 1,017 guitars shipped in 1963 to 1,704 in 1964 and 2,099 in 1965. In the meantime, sales of the Custom ($450) and Standard ($310) stayed relatively consistent, which goes to show that the explosion in sales was mostly due to newcomers picking up beginners' instruments to start a band in their garage. Those bands would pave the way for a new breed of guitar heroes that turned Gibson's older Les Paul into the Holy Grail of hard rock tone.

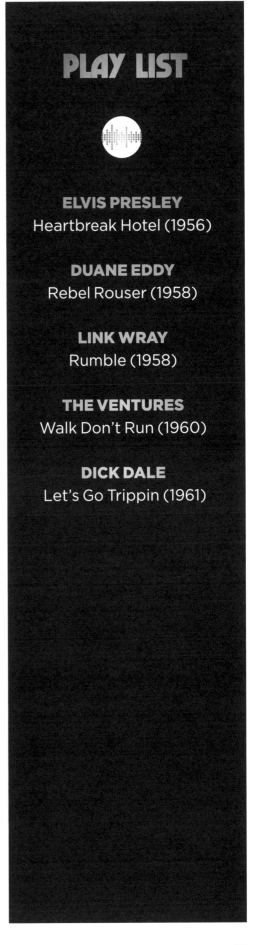

PLAY LIST

ELVIS PRESLEY
Heartbreak Hotel (1956)

DUANE EDDY
Rebel Rouser (1958)

LINK WRAY
Rumble (1958)

THE VENTURES
Walk Don't Run (1960)

DICK DALE
Let's Go Trippin (1961)

IT WAS JUST THE BEST GUITAR AVAILABLE AT THAT TIME. IT WAS MY FIRST TOUCH WITH A REALLY GREAT, CLASSIC ROCK 'N' ROLL ELECTRIC GUITAR, SO I FELL IN LOVE WITH THEM FOR A WHILE.

Keith Richards

GOD SAVE THE LES PAUL

The story of the Les Paul through the evolution of the guitars that bear this name is only half the story: those instruments would have never become such iconic objects if they had not been played on stage and on vinyl by the musicians who shaped popular music in the sixties. At that point, the story of this American guitar takes on a decidedly British accent.

FROM THE OTHER SIDE

Lonnie Donegan
in 1959 with what
appears to be a
Gretsch Duo Jet
with two Filter'Tron
humbuckers.

In the late fifties, skiffle was all the rage in Great Britain. That musical style found its origins in Southern US states in the 1920s, but it became another story once it was re-discovered by British jazz musicians in the fifties. Lonnie Donegan played the banjo in swing-jazz bands, and he created a hybrid style by incorporating US folk music and cheap makeshift instruments into his style. From the time he released his biggest hit, "Rock Island Line", in 1956, thousands of teens started playing the guitar, the banjo, or even the washboard and the washtub-bass to emulate his sound. In a pattern that would become recurring in the history of rock n' roll, skiffle was a simple music to play, musicians didn't need to be too proficient on their instrument and could quickly form a band with a few mates. They didn't even need to own an instrument, as they could build them at home. And if their parents were well-off, they could afford one of those cheap barely-playable archtop guitars that would instantly make you the leader of the band. "Rock Island Line" was a cover of a Leadbelly song, and the B-side was "John Henry", which was an even more dyed-in-the-wool American story. British musicians appropriating the US folklore was the start of a true musical dialogue back and forth between these two countries, a dialogue that keeps on defining the evolution of rock music to this day.

Among amateur skiffle players were people like Jimmy Page, Pete Townshend or John Lennon. Those youngsters were passionate about American culture, and would fully explore any US musical artifact they could get their hands on. Which were not that common back then: the post-war UK was still being rebuilt, and among other restrictions importing guitars from the US was banned until 1959. Plus of course information did not travel fast by today's standards; some albums had to be mail-ordered and you would finally get to listen to them a few weeks later. Sailors would sneak in a few rock n' roll records and even some American-made instruments, but those were still extremely hard to come-by.

In the early sixties, British musicians were becoming aware of the US musical revolution led by artists from the Motown, Chess and Sun labels, singers and guitarists like Chuck Berry, Gene Vincent, Little Richard and Buddy Holly, and bluesmen like Muddy Waters. But the gorgeous US guitars pictured on those records were virtually impossible to find on the other side of the pond, and British musicians had to make do with European-built brands like Hagstrom (made in Sweden), Futurama (Czech Republic), Hofner and Framus (Germany), Egmond (Holland), Eko (Italy), and a few English brands like Burns, Dallas and Watkins (mostly known for their amps, though they did a few guitars as well).

As the British Blues Boom started with bands like Alexis Korner's Blues Incorporated, British musicians were looking for that American sound, and a few of them started being seen with Gretsches and Telecasters. Les Pauls, however, were still an absolute rarity.

PATIENT ZERO

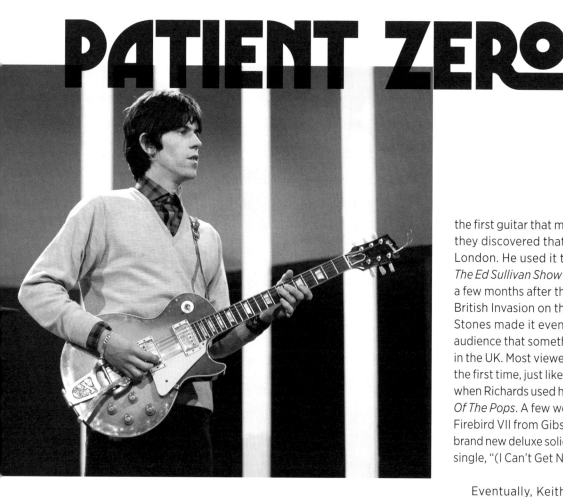

Keith Richards in March 1965 performing with the Burst on *Thank Your Lucky Stars*.

the first guitar that many Americans saw when they discovered that band of hoodlums from London. He used it to perform two songs on *The Ed Sullivan Show* in October 1964, and only a few months after the Beatles had started the British Invasion on the same show, the Rolling Stones made it even more obvious to the US audience that something special was going on in the UK. Most viewers were seeing a Burst for the first time, just like UK viewers in March 1965 when Richards used his Burst to perform on *Top Of The Pops*. A few weeks later, he purchased a Firebird VII from Gibson and started using that brand new deluxe solid body to record their next single, "(I Can't Get No) Satisfaction".

The first famous British musician who picked up a Les Paul and used it to spread the good word of rock n' roll was none other than Keith Richards in 1964. The Rolling Stones' human riff had only been playing hollow body guitars before that, first a cheaper Harmony Meteor and then an Epiphone Casino, the alternative version of the Gibson ES-330, a fully-hollow thinline instrument with two P90s built in Kalamazoo. Then, in August, right after the Stones had their first UK number one with "The Last Time", Richards bought a second-hand 1959 Les Paul Standard Sunburst that used to belong to John Bowen, a musician who had bought the guitar brand new in 1961. Bowen played in a band, and he had a Bigsby installed at Selmer's in London, not only a major music shop but also a great hang for musicians looking for like-minded people. Then, he traded it for a Gretsch, and that's how Richards got ahold of it.

Not only did it become Richards' main axe for a few very intense months, but it was also

Eventually, Keith sold the Burst in 1967. Swinging London was a small world at the time: before buying Keith's Burst, the buyer had bought his previous Les Paul from a salesman at Selmer called Paul Kossoff, who would later become a Burst-wielding legend in the band Free. That first Burst got stolen, so he was looking for a replacement. The buyer played in John Mayall's band, an outfit that turned the Burst into an object of desire. That buyer was none other than Mick Taylor, who would later join the Stones as a replacement for Brian Jones, so the original Keith Burst would become part of the Rolling Stones' arsenal for a second time in 1969. Small world indeed.

THE SECRET CUSTOM

The other pioneer of the Les Paul in England was a much more discreet character, namely Jimmy Page and his 1960 Les Paul Custom, complete with three gold-covered pickups and a golden Bigsby. He had bought it brand new in London a few months before Keith got his Burst, and the Black Beauty became his tool as a session player. From 1963 until 1967, Page was hired as a studio guitarist for many recordings, including songs for the Kinks, the Who, Shirley Bassey and countless others. All of Page's electric session work was done on the Custom. It had been modified with two extra toggle switches to get many combinations of the pickups, which allowed him to cover as much musical ground as possible with a single instrument. This was the time when most players, even pros, would own two or three guitars. The idea of a collection was not fully formed yet, since guitars were just tools and not luxurious historic items. When players wanted a new guitar, they would usually trade the other one in and fully commit to the newcomer. So even as a guitarist for hire who needed to play many different styles of music, it was not strange for Page to be doing all the work on a single Les Paul.

Session musicians of the time were not famous by any stretch of the imagination. Quite the opposite: they were never credited on album sleeves, and would often play on the record instead of the better-looking band members photographed on the cover. That is why very few pictures of Page with his Black Beauty exist: that sound is part of Britain's collective psyche at the time, but the guitar wasn't exposed to the public, and nobody bought a Les Paul following Page's example at the time.

Jimmy Page with the black Custom in the mid-sixties at the Selmer showroom.

PAGE'S STOLEN GUITAR

All of Jimmy Page's sixties session work was played on a 1960 Black Beauty Les Paul Custom with a Bigsby vibrato and three extra switches to get as many sounds as possible from this unique guitar. Unfortunately, that Custom was stolen during Led Zeppelin's fifth tour of North America in the Spring of 1970. On the 13th of April, the band took a plane to go from Minneapolis, Minnesota, to Montreal. The Custom did not cross the Canadian border, and it was nowhere to be found when the band landed.

Page was heartbroken, and he took an ad in *Rolling Stone* magazine every month for a year trying to find his beloved Custom. But it didn't happen.

In the early nineties, a man went to Willie's American Guitars in St. Paul, Minnesota, claiming he had Page's stolen guitar. Apparently, it was stolen by an airport employee who had kept it under his bed until he died, then his widow sold it. Nate Westgor, the owner of the store called a friend of Page's to check the guitar's authenticity, but it turns out it didn't have the three switches, and it didn't bear the mark of a refinish that would have been made after removing the said switches.

Therefore, the guitar was put up for sale as a regular 1960 Bigsby Les Paul Custom, which at the time was worth $5,000, and it was purchased by a store employee, young punk rocker Paul "Bleem" Claesgens. For twenty years, Bleem played the guitar on stage with his band Brass Elephant, and at some point removed the Bigsby to install a Tune-o-matic bridge.

At some point, he broke the neck and brought it back to Willie's American Guitars for a repair job. Westgor still had his doubts about the guitar being Page's, so he

inspected it with a black light torch and sure enough, he found the holes left by the missing switches. It turns out the guitar had been spectacularly well refinished to hide its shameful origin.

One detail was the final proof needed to identify it without the shadow of a doubt: on a live video of Page playing the guitar with Led Zeppelin, a dark stripe could be seen on the 12th fret inlay of the guitar, and the Minnesota Custom has the exact same stripe. This is how Page was finally reunited with his guitar in 2015, 45 years after losing it.

But Page wanted to tell the story in a spectacular way, so it was not made public until 2019, when the New York City Metropolitan Museum Of Art opened an exhibit of historic guitars. The Custom was there, proving that almost forty years after Led Zeppelin split, Page could still be a mysterious and fascinating character.

**JOHN MAYALL AND
THE BLUESBREAKERS**
BLUES BREAKERS
WITH ERIC CLAPTON
1966

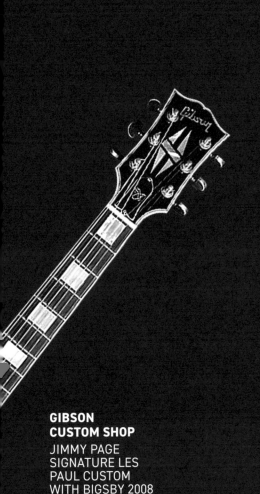

**GIBSON
CUSTOM SHOP**
JIMMY PAGE
SIGNATURE LES
PAUL CUSTOM
WITH BIGSBY 2008

On the other hand, there also was a friend of Page's playing a Les Paul that single-handedly turned it into the ultimate electric blues weapon. Jimmy Page, Eric Clapton and Jeff Beck were born within 15 months of each other in 1944 and 1945, and they all grew up in Surrey within 30 miles of each other, playing the guitar and listening to American blues and rockabilly. They became friends, and their careers have become inextricably linked.

Back in 1965, Eric Clapton left the British blues band The Yardbirds because he felt like they were heading in a pop direction. He had recommended Page as his replacement, but Jimmy was doing great as a session musician and didn't want to go back on the road with a touring band, so he recommended their friend Jeff Beck instead, who obviously got the gig.

Clapton then joined John Mayall & The Bluesbreakers, one of the pioneering blues bands in the country, and that's when he switched over from the Telecaster to the Les Paul.

Originally, Clapton was looking for another kind of Les Paul. He had fallen in love with the sound and look of Freddie King's Gold Top on the cover of *Let's Hide Away and Dance Away With Freddy King* (1962), but at the time a British customer couldn't just walk into a music shop and get a Gold Top. They would get whichever Les Paul was available, if any, and be content with it. In June 1965, the Les Paul that was available was to be Clapton's ultimate tone machine, the one Burst that defined how any Les Paul should sound, an elusive apparition that somehow had to disappear.

THE BEANO BURST

John Mayall's band The Bluesbreakers was just starting out: they had recorded their first album before Clapton joined, but the arrival of that new soloist turned the band into another animal altogether. Their music became extremely guitar-centric, almost as a jewel-case for Clapton's superhuman sound and playing. Nobody played like Clapton at the time, nobody had that sound, that feedback, that sustain, and that passion within each note. That was his magic hour: Clapton was freed from the pop format of the Yardbirds, he could express his deepest frustrations and was not yet burdened by egos and drugs in Cream. It is impossible to overstate the importance of Clapton's playing in 1965 and 1966: "Clapton is God" graffitis were popping up all over London, George Harrison was a fan, Jimi Hendrix was a fan, Duane Allman was a fan, and they all took hints from his approach.

Mayall himself wanted to display Clapton's playing to help promote his band, which is why he wanted to record his second album live to capture his guitarist's wild untamed side. But live recording was still an artform in its infancy at the time, and they decided they would get a better sound by going into a studio. In May 1966, Clapton brought his Burst and his Marshall amp to the Decca Studios and told the recording engineer it was going to be loud. The engineer in question was a young Jimmy Page who was also working as a producer in those days. The rest is history: no other guitarist had captured such a juicy, fat and lively distorted sound on tape before, including a blistering cover of the signature Freddie King instrumental "Hideaway", the song that convinced Clapton to get a Les Paul. Mayall knew what he had too: his guitar player's name was part of the name of the album, called *John Mayall - Bluesbreakers with Eric Clapton*. Even though he went on to host many brilliant players in his band, no one else would get that honor. Since then, the Clapton album has been nicknamed "The Beano Album" since the guitarist, always friendly and sociable, can be seen reading a *Beano* comic on the front cover.

Eric Clapton plays a Burst next to a Marshall stack with Cream in 1966. By that time, the Beano Burst is already gone, and Clapton has borrowed the Keith Burst for that show, hence the Bigsby.

Not much was said at the time on how Clapton got that sound, and players just had to guess. The back cover was not much to go by: Clapton could be seen tuning a Les Paul but the guitar wasn't clearly visible. The amp on the other hand was well-exposed, and the album was great publicity for Marshall at the time. Jim Marshall was a drummer who started building amps in his London store in 1963, and the 1962 model (not to be confused with the year) was a 35-watt combo based on Marshall's JTM-45 head. That first pairing of PAF pickups into a cranked-up Marshall still rings as the gold standard for rock guitar tone today, and many other players would go on to try and replicate the formula.

The back cover of the Bluesbreakers album, on which the Beano Burst can barely be seen.

Clapton's Burst was stolen in the summer of 1966. By then, he had left Mayall's band, and he was rehearsing with his new band, Cream. Clapton would go on to own and borrow many other guitars, including a Burst with a Bigsby, a cherry red ES-335 and a psychedelic-painted SG, but he never got that sound again. To this day, the Beano Burst is still missing, and very few pictures exist that would help define its specs. Clapton doesn't remember if it was a 1959 or a 1960 Les Paul (no one cared about that at the time), the only clues we have are the patterns of the maple top and the exposed PAFs. Clapton removed the pickup covers to get more treble out of the guitar (a trick many other players would use), so it seems that the bridge pickup was black and the neck pickup was cream.

The fact that this magical guitar got stolen only added to its mythical aura: if Clapton still had the guitar, he probably wouldn't sound the same as in 1966. The fact that it's gone means that the magic can never be replicated and the original moment remains special and untouched. Keith Richards was a Burst pioneer, but Clapton is the one who showed the way for so many players, and turned the Les Paul into a must-have guitar for any serious soloist in the late-sixties.

GIBSON CUSTOM SHOP
LES PAUL ERIC CLAPTON "BEANO" '60 LES PAUL 2011

IN ABSENTIA

Stolen guitars have been the plague of sixties and seventies rock stars, and many significant instruments have vanished without being found. But some of those guitars are so important and have been so instrumental in the history of rock that Gibson had no choice but to replicate them *in absentia*. They did exactly that for three major Les Pauls: Peter Frampton's Custom in 2000, Jimmy Page's Custom in 2008 and Eric Clapton's Burst in 2010. Those replicas made by the Custom Shop were based on photographs of the original instruments and what the players could remember from their guitar a few decades later. They might not be as accurate as some replicas of guitars that were scanned and thoroughly inspected, but they represent some of the most iconic Les Pauls that ever were, and that symbol is strong enough to make the replicas iconic in their own right.

The Frampton "Phenix" was finally found in 2012, and the Page Black Beauty was rediscovered in 2015. But to this day, the Beano Burst is still missing. That 1960 Burst was stolen from Clapton in the summer of 1966 while he was rehearsing with Cream. Very little is known about it since Clapton had only owned it for a year, the year during which he changed the face of music with John Mayall and the Bluesbreakers.

Clapton never wrote down the serial number, so it is impossible to know if the guitar actually is a 1960 or a 1959 model. Pictures with the covers removed show a double white PAF in the neck position and a double black in the bridge position, a relatively plain top, and Clapton remembers the neck as being slim, which would indicate a 1960 model, but it doesn't prove much so long after the fact.

**GIBSON
CUSTOM SHOP**
LES PAUL PETER
FRAMPTON

500 replicas were built by the Gibson Custom Shop in 2010, and in 2017 Joe Bonamassa caused quite a stir when he said that he knew the whereabouts of the guitar, and that it was with a private guitar collector on the US East Coast. Until the guitar actually surfaces, this is only hearsay. But as Frampton and Page's Customs have shown, it is never too late to be reunited with your long-lost love.

THEN PLAY ON

Mayall was quick to find a replacement for Clapton, since he remembered a young gunslinger who had already replaced Clapton for four gigs in October 1965. Peter Allen Greenbaum, aka Peter Green, was nineteen years old when he joined the Bluesbreakers in 1966, and even though he had huge shoes to fill, his playing made him a worthy replacement. Just like Clapton, he had a Burst, a '59 with funny pickups. As Green himself explained: "I never had a magic Les Paul... It was an old-fashioned one with a funny-shaped neck - a kind of semicircle neck. It just barely worked. The pickups were strong, but I took one of them off. I copied Eric Clapton. I heard him play one night, and he was on the treble pickups all night long. It sounded so good.

I thought I'd take my bass pickup off altogether. Try and wait for the same luck. But I put it back on the wrong way around so that the poles - the pickup screws - were facing in the opposite direction. (...) People would say that I got a special sound and try to force me to agree, but I don't think so."

Green saying his Les Paul wasn't magical is understandable: this is a quote from a semi-retired musician fighting with mental health issues who parted with his Burst a long time ago and is tired of people mentioning it to him. He also raises an interesting point that should always be kept in mind when talking about legendary guitars: a guitar is only as good as the person playing it. Clapton would've sounded amazing on any guitar in 1966, and a mediocre player would still sound uninspired if they were playing the Beano Burst. In this way, there is no magic Les Paul indeed.

Green mentions his neck pickup being the wrong way around, and it is clear on any picture that its pole pieces are pointing towards the bridge pickup instead of the neck. But according to Joel Dantzig, founder of Hamer guitars who inspected the guitar a few years later, that misplacement didn't change the sound. Peter Green's famous thin fluting sound that he would get in the middle position with both pickups on can be explained by a faulty wiring at the factory. The pickups were wired out of phase with each other, hence that special sound that many players have tried to replicate since then.

With that Les Paul, Peter Green recorded *A Hard Road* with John Mayall in 1967, then he left to form his own band, Fleetwood Mac, with the help of former Mayall alumni Mick Fleetwood on the drums and John McVie on the bass. Backed by guitarists Jeremy Spencer and Danny Kirwan (a Les Paul enthusiast himself), Peter Green's creativity, touch and sound were unparalleled

JOHN MAYALL AND THE BLUESBREAKERS
A HARD ROAD
1967

Peter Green playing his '59 Burst with Fleetwood Mac at the Royal Albert Hall in 1969.

GIBSON CUSTOM SHOP
COLLECTOR'S CHOICE #1 MELVYN FRANKS' '59 LES PAUL STANDARD REISSUE

GARY MOORE
STILL GOT THE
BLUES
1990

on the first three albums of his band: *Fleetwood Mac, Mr Wonderful* and *Then Play On*. In 1970, due to his inner struggles, he had to step down and let Fleetwood Mac exist without him. At that point, he sold his Burst to a young fan, Irish guitarist Gary Moore, who named it "Greeny" as a tribute to its former owner and used it with the band Thin Lizzy as well as for his solo career, including the classic 1978 ballad "Parisienne Walkways".

The guitar had its neck broken in a car accident, and in the late eighties, Gary Moore bought another '59 Burst nicknamed Stripe. Apparently, he prefered the sound of "Stripe", and this is the one pictured on the cover of Moore's "back-to-his-blues-roots" 1990 *Still Got The Blues* album (played by a kid version of Moore plugged into a Marshall Bluesbreaker combo, as it should be). But in 2006, Moore had to cancel a tour because of a hand injury, which put him in need of a large amount of cash, so he ended up selling Greeny. The guitar then went through several private collectors for astronomical sums, and it was replicated by Gibson in 2010 as the first of their new Collector's Choice series under the name of its owner at the time, Melvyn Franks. Then, in July 2014, its owner needed cash, and sold Greeny to a longtime fan of Gary Moore and the late Peter Green, Kirk Hammett of Metallica. Since then, Hammett has been using it in the studio and even brings it out on stage for his band's monstrous world tours, still rocking it 55 years after Peter Green's stint with John Mayall.

Gary Moore playing Peter Green's Burst live in 1995. The tell-tale signs are the unmatched knobs and the neck humbucker's pole pieces facing towards the bridge.

COLLECTING AND MODDING

After Green left the Bluesbreakers, Mayall replaced him with yet another Burst genius, eighteen year-old Mick Taylor. He used the Keith Burst to record the fourth John Mayall album, *Crusade*, in July 1967, before he finally joined The Rolling Stones in 1969. At that point, he bought another Burst, a '59 with a plain top and two screw holes left by a removed Bigsby vibrato. The removed pickup covers showed two black humbuckers, and this is the guitar in Charlie Watt's left hand on the cover of the 1970 live album, *Get Yer Ya-Ya's Out*. Then, in 1971, the Rolling Stones went to the South of France to record what would become *Exile on Main St.*, and Richards brought his new toy, another '59 Burst with a more intense flame top than the other. Together, Richards and Taylor owned three Bursts among many other cool guitars, including Customs and a Bigsby-equipped SG.

When Clapton left The Yardbirds, his friend Jeff Beck stepped in to replace him. At that point, the notoriously moody and utterly brilliant Beck had a Fender Esquire modified with a contoured body. In late 1966, shocked by Clapton's sound on the Bluesbreakers album, he bought a 1958 Les Paul with a dark sunburst at Selmer's. This was his main guitar for the remainder of his stint with the Yardbirds (before Jimmy Page took over after a brief period with those two as dueling lead players), and this is also the Les Paul used for his groundbreaking debut album with the Jeff Beck Group, *Truth* (1968). At that point, Beck was taking Clapton's approach even further, finding new and more oblique sounds every time he played. He proceeded to remove the pickup covers on this first Burst, which revealed two double whites, and then took off

THE ROLLING STONES
GET YER YA-YA'S OUT!
1970

JEFF BECK
BLOW BY BLOW
1975

THE JEFF BECK GROUP
TRUTH
1968

the sunburst finish completely in order to get the full unhampered resonance of the wood. That natural finish was becoming fashionable at the time, and many other players would sand off their guitars to get closer to their best possible sound, including John Lennon and his Epiphone Casino or Mick Ronson and his Les Paul Custom.

In 1968, that Burst had its headstock broken by a roadie after a concert in Chicago. Rick Nielsen was in the audience, and he was already into collecting older Gibsons but was yet to become the founder of Cheap Trick. Nielsen got in touch with Beck's team and brought him five guitars to choose from. Beck picked number 91864, a '59 Burst with a particularly spectacular flame top that he paid $350 for, which was already a hefty sum at the time (as Nielsen says: "that's what they went for back then, they were hard to find... I'd traded about two months earlier an SG and $25 to get that one").

But then that Burst got stolen, and while on tour in Memphis in the early seventies, Beck found his ultimate Les Paul at the Strings & Things store: a 1954 wraparound Gold Top that had been heavily modified with two humbuckers, new tuners and a deep dark oxblood color. That guitar would have been a piece of junk to a lot of players looking for an original Burst or even an untouched Gold Top, but this is the one Beck chose for his best instrumental albums of the era, including *Blow By Blow* (with the Oxblood Les Paul on the cover). In 2009, that guitar was replicated by the Gibson Custom Shop.

Those mods were not unusual at the time, since those Les Pauls were not sacred

untouchable collector's items, but simple tools that needed to serve a purpose. Neil Young's Old Black is a 1953 Gold Top painted black with a Bigsby and a Firebird bridge pickup. He got the guitar in 1968 as he was starting his solo career and he's still playing it out on the road today. Frank Zappa's 1952 Gold Top has had a Telecaster pickup added next to the uncovered original bridge P90, plus a Bigsby and a neck humbucker, and he used it extensively on the *Hot Rats* album (1969).

Perhaps the most famous modified Les Paul was "Lucy". It started its life as a 1957 Gold Top (the humbucker version) that was bought by John Sebastian of the New York band The Lovin' Spoonful. It may have been bought as a spare guitar for Sebastian's Burst, but it ended up being sold in 1966.

Rick Derringer was playing in The McCoys when he got the guitar. They had released a massive hit the previous year with "Hang On Sloopy". It had a Bigsby installed and was pretty beat-up, and since Rick lived close to Kalamazoo, he took the Gold Top to the Gibson factory and had it refinished in the Cherry Red that was popular on the SGs of the era. This is probably when it lost its Bigsby. The refinished guitar didn't sound and feel as good to Derringer, so he traded it at a New York store for a Burst. Clapton bought it there, and he gave it to George Harrison in August 1968, a few weeks before Clapton used it to record his solo on "While My Guitar Gently Weeps". Harrison nicknamed the Les Paul Lucy in reference to the red-haired Lucille Ball, and it became his main guitar for the remainder of the Beatles' recording career, on *The Beatles*

George Harrison playing "Lucy" during his North American tour in 1974.

GIBSON CUSTOM SHOP
JEFF BECK SIGNATURE '54 LES PAUL REISSUE

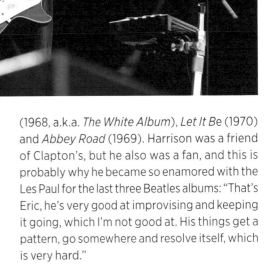

(1968, a.k.a. *The White Album*), *Let It Be* (1970) and *Abbey Road* (1969). Harrison was a friend of Clapton's, but he also was a fan, and this is probably why he became so enamored with the Les Paul for the last three Beatles albums: "That's Eric, he's very good at improvising and keeping it going, which I'm not good at. His things get a pattern, go somewhere and resolve itself, which is very hard."

Above
Neil Young live in the late 2010s, still rocking Old Black.

Left
Jeff Beck in the early seventies playing his 1954 modified Gold Top with humbuckers and Oxblood finish.

EARLY BLOOMER

**GIBSON
CUSTOM SHOP**

MICHAEL
BLOOMFIELD
'59 LES PAUL
STANDARD

The previously aforementioned John Sebastian was the first major Burst convert in the US. As soon as The Lovin' Spoonful started touring back in 1965, the Burst was there, and it made Sebastian a true anomaly in a folk rock scene that was more used to Fenders and Gretsches. It can be heard on all of their hits, including "Do You Believe in Magic" and "Summer In The City". Sebastian kept this beautiful flame top '59 for years after the Spoonful's breakup, before he finally sold it in the nineties. It has also been replicated by the Gibson Custom Shop as Collector's Choice #13 in 2014.

Sebastian was not a virtuoso, and therefore he didn't do as much as Clapton or Beck to reveal the guitar's sonic possibilities, but he passed the bug on to a true guitar genius who in turn made the Burst even more desirable. Sebastian was friends with the producer of the Paul Butterfield Blues Band, and this is how he ended up spending time with one of the two guitar players from that Chicago electric blues band, Mike Bloomfield. Bloomfield had already been part of history by recording guitar on Bob Dylan's career-defining 1965 album *Highway 61 Revisited*, but by the time he met Sebastian he had stopped playing his blonde Telecaster

and was enamored with a wraparound Gold Top. But then he saw Sebastian's Burst: "He loved it, and the next time we crossed paths, he showed me a much more dramatic instrument with a lot more curl! For years after that, our conversations began with talk about Les Pauls. And he was a lead player, so he knew how to get the best sounds from an instrument."

Bloomfield was a lead player indeed. As Clapton famously said: "Bloomfield is music on two legs", and when he started playing on his Burst, beautiful exotic blues would flow from his fingers. His Burst was a '59 model with gorgeous flames, which he traded for his Gold Top plus a hundred bucks with guitar tech Dan Erlewine. It was replicated by the Gibson Custom Shop in 2009 as the '59 Bloomfield Burst.

After he left the Butterfield Band, Bloomfield formed the Electric Flag, but after one great album, the aptly named *A Long Time Comin'* (1968), Bloomfield got together with organist Al Kooper (who had also played on the Dylan album), and they started jamming in the studio to capture their utter brilliance as improvisators. After a first day of recording, Bloomfield went back home, crippled by insomnia. For the second day, Kooper called Stephen Stills who stepped in at the last minute to replace Bloomfield. The resulting album, *Super Session* (1968), is a hodgepodge of fiddling about and moments of true grace, including Bloomfield's tribute to John Coltrane, "His Holy Modal Majesty".

Bloomfield was a true genius, but not unlike Peter Green he was ill-equipped to deal with

THE ELECTRIC FLAG

A LONG TIME COMIN'

1968

FREE

TONS OF SOBS

1968

The Electric Flag playing live at the Bitter End club in New York in 1967. From left to right: Mike Bloomfield and his Burst, Buddy Miles on the drums (who will go on to play in Hendrix's Band Of Gypsys) and Harvey Brooks on the Fender bass.

the pressure and grind of a musician's life on the road. This partly explains why he's not as much of a household name as he should be, but his playing has influenced anybody who's been lucky enough to have crossed his path, and he turned the Burst into the ultimate lead instrument in America.

In the UK meanwhile, another fine blues player was also making the transition towards the Burst. Paul Kossoff was a salesman at Selmer's, and he wanted a Burst after seeing Clapton on stage with the Bluesbreakers. He was only seventeen years old when he formed the band Free, and eighteen when they released their 1968 debut album, *Tons of Sobs*, which features an intense cover of Albert King's "The Hunter", complete with Kossoff's trademark searing bends. He is one of the early proponents of the magical "Burst-on-a-Marshall-stack" formula, even though he sometimes used early Orange amps (which had a more prominent upper-midrange than the Marshalls).

He started off with a TV Junior, then got a 1955 Custom, which he traded for a beautiful 1960 Standard with tiger stripes, the *Tons of Sobs* guitar. He also had a 1957 three-pickup Custom, which he traded with Clapton in 1969 for a 1958 Burst. This Standard had a very recognizable dark sunburst, and since it used to belong to Kossoff's idol, it remained his main Les Paul for the remainder of his short career, before his tragic death in 1976 at the age of 25. He also had a beautiful 1959 Standard whose neck got broken and repaired. This one bears a big scratch between the two pickups on the treble side, and it has been replicated in 2012 as the Paul Kossoff '59 Les Paul. He also owned a Les Paul with a stripped-down finish which he famously played at the Isle of Wight festival in 1970.

Kossoff had a unique playing style, a magnificent sound and a taste for using the full dynamic range of his instrument that defined what a good Les Paul could do in a high-headroom amp. His vibrato was wonderfully vocal, and it was a major influence on many greats from Angus Young to Joe Bonamassa.

Paul Kossoff playing with Free at the Isle of Wight Festival on 30th August 1970. His Les Paul has been sanded down to a natural finish and he's standing in front of several Marshall stacks.

PLAY LIST

THE ROLLING STONES
Little Red Rooster (1964)

JOHN MAYALL AND THE BLUESBREAKERS WITH ERIC CLAPTON
Hideaway (1966)

JEFF BECK
Beck's Bolero (1968)

BLOOMFIELD
His Holy Modal Majesty (1968)

FLEETWOOD MAC
Albatross (1969)

FREE
Fire And Water (1970)

GARY MOORE
Still Got The Blues (1990)

OKAY, YOU WIN. WE ARE PLEASED TO ANNOUNCE THAT MORE OF THE ORIGINAL LES PAUL GIBSONS ARE AVAILABLE. LINE FORMS AT YOUR GIBSON DEALER'S.

1968 Gibson ad

THE LES PAUL IS BACK

There is a stark contrast between the general fascination for the Les Paul starting in the mid-sixties and the sorry state of Gibson as a company during that same period of time. While the guitars they used to manufacture were selling for more and more steep prices on the used market, business was not that great anymore after the 1965 peak, due to exterior as well as interior factors.

OUT OF TOUCH

1965 Gibson ad featuring Tal Farlow, Johnny Smith and Barney Kessel.

First things first, general sales of guitars started decreasing from 1966 on, which seems logical. The peak was the result of many beginners trying their hands at a new instrument after having seen the Beatles on national TV in 1964. But such a cultural landslide could never be reproduced at such a massive scale, it was a unique moment in American and British History and would remain so. Secondly, Gibson was hurt by truckers going on strike in the Chicago area, which ended up becoming a nationwide truckers strike in 1967. It was a problem both to get materials to build the guitars, and then to send those guitars to dealers once they were built. A strike also took place at the Gibson factory in 1966, during which workers stopped building instruments for no less than sixteen days.

The many extra guitars that had to be built to meet the demand were not necessarily done with the attention to detail they deserved, and quality control issues were starting to appear. Ted McCarty left Gibson in 1966 and, after a few short stints, the next significant president of the company was Stan Rendell in early 1968. Rendell later described the situation when he arrived on board: "We had all kinds of quality problems. We had production problems. We had personnel problems. We had union problems. We had problems that wouldn't end." But on top of all that, Gibson had a true problem getting in tune with the trends of the era. They were a company run by older gentlemen who thought the electric guitar was just a passing fad, and who had no idea people like Clapton, Beck and Page even existed.

Instead of catering to these new guitar heroes, Gibson was designing signature models for

jazz players who obviously did not spark the same interest as British Invasion artists. They were great musicians, but not great sellers and not great marketing operations for Gibson. In 1961, Gibson released the Johnny Smith (a D'Angelico-inspired archtop) and two Barney Kessel models, the Regular and the Custom, both archtops with two florentine cutaways. Tal Farlow was next in 1962, with yet another archtop featuring a mandolin-style scroll on the cutaway, and two models were added for Trini Lopez in 1964, the Deluxe (basically a Barney Kessel Regular with a Fender-like headstock) and the Standard (an ES-335 with diamond-shaped f-holes and Fender-like headstock). All those models were gorgeous displays of what Gibson could do, but none of them was in touch with the music of teenagers, apart from the fact that Johnny Smith wrote "Walk Don't Run" which became a hit for The Ventures!

1967 Gibson ad featuring Barney Kessel "at work for Contemporary Records".

Barney Kessel & Gibson at work for Contemporary Records.

Three sixties Gibson
signature guitars from the
collection of musician Andy
Reiss: Tal Farlow 1963, Trini
Lopez Deluxe 1968 , Barney
Kessel 1966.

MORE OF *Les*

1968 Gibson ad for the Custom and Gold Top reissues, featuring the infamous "Okay You Win" text.

The fact that Gibson wasn't aware of the musical trends of the day explains how long it took for them to start producing Les Pauls again. Back then, musicians would write to music magazines because they wanted a Custom and couldn't get one, and a lot of players didn't even know Gibson had stopped making them. That was the beginning of the vintage market as we know it today: word was out that the Les Paul was a great guitar, and more and more artists were using it, everybody wanted a piece of the Clapton / Bloomfield sound, but since they were not readily available you had to pay top dollar for a good one. Les Paul had released a new album in 1967, the first since 1962, with a title that seemed to sum up what guitar players were asking from Gibson: *Les Paul Now*. The time was right, even slightly overdue, and at the 1968 Summer NAMM Show the new Les Paul models were introduced. Even the ad of the time admits that Gibson did it reluctantly ("Okay, you win"), and they reissued the "wrong" models, which goes to show how deeply out of touch they were at the time. Instead of reissuing the obvious Burst that was getting significant attention from many serious players, they chose to make a 1955-style Gold Top (named Standard to make things more confusing) and a 1958-style Black Beauty Custom with two humbuckers instead of the original three-pickup model. Originally, Gibson wanted to make the Custom white to match the SG Custom, but the factory had a problem with white paint, so they decided to paint it black.

Those reissues were great guitars, and they were surprisingly close to the originals: Gibson had been smart enough not to mess with a good thing, and to this day those first-year reissues are highly coveted by collectors and musicians alike, the only tell-tale sign being their knobs, which are reflectors for the Gold Top and witch-hat for the Custom. That Custom was hiding a big twist under its black paint, however: it had a maple top. Contrary to the original Black Beauties of the fifties, the Custom had the same body construction as a Standard or a Gold Top, with a maple top on a mahogany body. This made a significant difference soundwise, and it explains why a lot of musicians have gravitated towards those reissues rather than the originals, even back when the price difference was not that significant.

But very soon, compromises were made to the detriment of the guitar's quality. In 1969, in spite of its commercial success, the Gold Top was discontinued, probably to make way for the new Deluxe. The Custom's body on the other hand was changed to a pancake construction, meaning a sandwich of woods with a thin maple layer between two layers of mahogany. This would allow Gibson to use smaller chunks of wood, which was coherent with the cost-cutting decisions of their new owner, Norlin. Norlin was a new company born in 1969 when ECL, a South-American brewing conglomerate (run by Norton Stevens, hence the "Nor" part of the Norlin name), bought CMI (and founder Maurice Berlin, hence the "lin" part). This was the last great acquisition of the sixties: because of the mid-sixties boom, large conglomerates thought there was big money to be made in the music business. Fender was bought by CBS in 1965, Gretsch by Baldwin in 1967, and Gibson CMI by Norlin in 1969. Those three buyouts produced very similar results: companies that used to be run by people who thought of instruments and musicians were now run by more business-minded people who wanted to produce those instruments for the lowest price. Corners had to be cut, both in materials (lower-quality heavier woods were bought) and in personnel (builders had to do more with less time).

Those changes have resulted in the seventies being kind of a "lost decade" for the bigger brands, with strange models and not-quite-right reissues of classics. Eventually, this led to more and more players turning to the vintage market.

GIBSON
LES PAUL CUSTOM
1971

GIBSON
LES PAUL
STANDARD
1969

The Custom is sporting
the original "witch
hat" knobs, and the
placement of the logo
on the Gold Top's
headstock is high
as can be.

THE LAST TIME

JOHN FOGERTY
PREMONITION
1998

Artists were not that quick to jump on those Les Paul reissues: most of them had already found the vintage guitar they were looking for, and they usually wanted a Burst rather than a Gold Top or a two-pickup Custom.

Among the notable exceptions is Brian Jones of the Rolling Stones. In December 1968, the band decided to bring together the best British Invasion artists, including themselves, and film a performance for television. They decided to call that televised festival *The Rock and Roll Circus*, but it was not broadcast at the time, since the Stones were not pleased with their performance, especially compared with newcomers like Jethro Tull or Taj Mahal. However, a recent DVD release of that concert shows Brian Jones playing a 1968 Gold Top "Standard". This would be Jones' last public appearance with the Stones before he was fired and died the following year: the last guitar played in public by the founder of the Rolling Stones was a 1968 Gold Top Les Paul.

On the other side of the stage, Keith Richards had a Custom for that show, a three-pickup late-fifties Black Beauty acquired in 1966, modified with a psychedelic painting on the front in 1967. At the time, more and more players were getting hip to the absolute class of an old Custom. Hendrix could be seen playing a '54-style Alnico V model when he wasn't playing one of his Strats, and King Crimson's leader Robert Fripp had a beautiful three-pickup '59 model with the covers removed that showed a zebra PAF in the neck position.

Robby Krieger from the L.A. band The Doors was also a Custom enthusiast. His main squeeze was an SG, but he bought a 1954 Custom in 1968

and used it exclusively for the slide parts. He removed the original Bigsby and also replaced the neck Alnico V pickup with a mini humbucker. This is the final form of the guitar that was picked for its replica by the Gibson Custom Shop in 2014.

Finally, the singer/solo guitarist and main songwriter for a dashing new band from California, Creedence Clearwater Revival, had played on a Lennon-like Rickenbacker for his first two albums, but from 1969 on (starting with the fat and crunchy "Bad Moon Rising"), John Fogerty played a 1968 reissue Black Beauty. He is

one of those rare artists from the era who really made the two-humbucker look work for him, to the point that it has become hard to picture him without his trusty Custom.

GIBSON CUSTOM SHOP

ROBBY KRIEGER '54 LES PAUL CUSTOM

The Rolling Stones performing on *The Rock And Roll Circus*, 11th December 1968. From Left to right: Brian Jones and his 1968 Gold Top reissue, Mick Jagger (vocals), Rocky Dzidzornu (maracas), Charlie Watts (drums), Keith Richards with his three-pickup Custom painted in psychedelic motifs, Bill Wyman (bass).

LUXURY LINER

Pete Townshend from
The Who performing
at Madison Square
Garden (New York)
on March 11, 1976.
He is playing his #4
modified Gold Top
Deluxe.

Production of the Gold Top reissue was stopped as early as 1969, only a few months after it had started. Dealers wanted a sunburst guitar with humbuckers instead of that Gold Top with P90s, and Gibson was happy to oblige. Kind of. They had already routed plenty of bodies for the P90s of the Gold Top, and they didn't want to waste time rerouting them for humbuckers. Plus they had a lot of leftover Epiphone mini humbuckers. Those pickups would equip models like the Coronet and Riviera, but since sales of the Epiphone brand were dwindling down (mostly due to the fact that they were about the same price as their Gibson equivalents), there were a lot of those pickups left by the time Gibson decided to turn Epiphone into their offshore-production brand.

A cream pickup ring was added, and those mini humbuckers could be fitted in P90 cavities. And just like that, the Deluxe was born. That model was the first proper new Les Paul model in a very long time, but it was not what players had in mind. The first ones were made in Gold Top only, but soon they were also available in a few other colors, including sunburst (at last!). But those mini humbuckers sounded nothing like PAFs, they were more aggressive and shrill, plus these Deluxes with their pancake bodies would weigh much more than your typical Burst. Also, the maple tops were not necessarily

GIBSON
LES PAUL DELUXE
1972

GIBSON
GOLD TOP DELUXE
1969

This 1969 Gold Top Deluxe has been converted to a Standard with a sunburst finish, two T-Top humbuckers and an extra Gretsch-style master volume on the cutaway.

Note the wear caused by years of using the volume knob.

Note the three-piece top and the embossed pickup covers with the Gibson logo, which were only available in 1972.

Headstocks of the seventies were much larger than they used to be.

THE LES PAUL IS BACK

**SOCIAL
DISTORTION**

SOMEWHERE
BETWEEN HEAVEN
AND HELL

1992

1979 ad for The Who's
soundtrack album *The
Kids Are Alright*.

GIBSON
LES PAUL PETE
TOWNSHEND
SIGNATURE

bookmatched with a center seam, which, along with a shade of sunburst that was a little too red, didn't make them as cosmetically appealing as the older Standards.

Over time though, those guitars have become classics in their own right, true symbols of the seventies and great instruments if you use them for what they are, i.e. not a substitute for a Burst. Pete Townshend from The Who was one of the first to get hip to the Deluxe, after having performed for years with a simple SG Special. He needed guitars he could break and repair without sacrificing a priceless rarity, and the Deluxe fit the bill perfectly. He started using them in late 1971, and they became his main touring guitars from 1973 until 1979. In 1975, he started modding them to fit his needs by putting a DiMarzio Super Distortion humbucker in the middle position between the two mini humbuckers, which gave his guitars a very recognizable look that has become iconic. An extra switch would activate that extra pickup, and another switch would put it out of phase with the other two. He would travel with six to eight of them, most of them Gold Top and all of them numbered with huge white numbers on the top: 1 and 5 were Wine Red, 2, 3, 4 and 6 were Gold Tops (2 and 6 remained unmodded), 8 and 9 were Sunburst. Some of those have been replicated as limited runs by the Gibson Custom Shop: #5 in 2001, #1, #3 and #9 in 2005, and an unnumbered Gold Top in 2016.

The Super Distortion humbucker, made by Staten Island company DiMarzio, was the first aftermarket pickup available, which meant that players didn't have to take their humbuckers from a guitar to put them in another anymore. That market quickly took off, helped by the fact that the Super Distortion had twice the output

level of a regular PAF and ceramic magnets, all of which would result in a big crunchy distortion from any kind of amp. From that point on, many vintage Deluxes were modded to accommodate two regular-sized humbuckers and convert them to Standard-ish specs. Mike Ness from the California punk band Social Distortion is the other player known for his heavy use of a Deluxe. Ironically, his 1976 Deluxe has been modded with two cream P90s instead of the mini humbuckers, bringing it back to pre-Deluxe specs. It is beautifully displayed on the cover of the 1992 classic album *Somewhere Between Heaven and Hell*, where Mike Ness is pictured mid-jump, in a very Townshend-esque pose. That guitar was replicated by the Gibson Custom Shop in 2022.

123

LES PAUL'S LES PAULS

1971 ad for the Les Paul Recording.

As part of the negotiations that took place in 1967 to bring Les Paul back into the fold, the guitarist and inventor brought up his personal preference for low impedance pickups. That choice was turned into two models in 1969, the Les Paul Personal and the Les Paul Professional. They shared a very complex array of knobs and switches, including an 11-position Decade switch (a tone filter), another tone switch and a phase switch, plus a three-band EQ. They were both finished in natural walnut, but the Personal had the more luxurious Custom-style inlays (including the split diamond on the headstock) and the gold hardware, plus it even had an XLR input with its own dedicated volume knob to plug a microphone.

But the big defining feature for the two models were those large slanted low impedance pickups. In layman terms, low impedance means that a broader spectrum is picked up and transmitted to the amp, but the signal needs a booster to be properly used with a regular amp. With high impedance pickups like PAFs or P90s, the sound loses treble and punch as it goes through lengthy cables and less-than-transparent pedals. This can be a desired effect for a player who's trying to tame the shrillness of a large amp like the Marshall plexi. The Professional and Personal had to be used with a supplied special cable that included the booster in order to be played through any amp, but Gibson also sold matching amps with the right input impedance to be using those pickups with a regular cable (the monstrous solid-state LP-12). Les Paul himself didn't have that problem, since he mostly used those pickups straight into a recording console, which was perfect to get that strong bright high-end he was after. As a guitarist, Les Paul

wanted a brighter sound and he didn't like that dull darker sound that had become de rigueur in jazz. As an engineer, he didn't understand why high impedance had become standard:"I always built my own pickups, or altered the ones Gibson gave me. This is because I figured out very early through my study of electronics that low impedance was the way to go. If you walked into a professional recording studio and someone handed you a high-impedance mic, you'd think he was nuts. High-impedance pickups are the industry standard simply because they're cheaper. You wind the coil, and go directly into the tube or transistor. With low impedance, you need a transformer to transform the energy from low to high at the amplifier. But with high-impedance pickups, every foot of cord adds capacitance, and knocks down the high frequencies. That should have been pretty obvious. Unfortunately, we started in the music industry with high impedance, locked ourselves in, and, for some reason, we haven't turned ourselves around."

To this day, high impedance remains standard, even though a few tone-obsessed players have been toying with the idea of low impedance through buffers and boosters, like Jerry Garcia (The Grateful Dead), Frank Zappa and Pink Floyd's David Gilmour (who at some point even had an XLR output installed on his main Strat). The California brand EMG has developed a range of "active" pickups, i.e. low impedance pickups with a booster powered by a battery, and those have been really popular with studio musicians in the eighties and metal players after that.

The Personal and Professional were not a resounding success, and they probably were not helped by their prohibitive price: the Professional cost $485 while the Deluxe cost $425, the Custom cost $575, and the Personal cost an astounding $645. But they were probably not meant as smashing best-sellers. These two guitars were a way for Les Paul to have his real personal model featuring everything he actually needed. The original Les Paul Model was a Gibson design with Les Paul's name on it, while the Les Paul Personal was Les Paul's design with Gibson's name on it. It was the evolution of the Logs and clunkers, and Les Paul ended up using it for most of his life when he performed.

Incidentally, those two were not the craziest designs introduced in the Les Paul line in 1969: there was the Les Paul Jumbo acoustic, a cutaway dreadnought with a low-impedance pickup and a decade switch. Needless to say that design wasn't a hit. Neither was the low-impedance equipped Les Paul Bass, which evolved into the Triumph Bass.

The Personal and Professional were replaced with the Les Paul Recording in 1971. It had the same walnut and split-diamond look as the Personal, but chrome-plated hardware like the Professional. The pickups and controls were the same, but they were presented in a slightly more accessible fashion. To this day, Terry Kath from Chicago remains the only high-profile user of those low-impedance pickups with a Les Paul Professional.

GIBSON
LES PAUL
RECORDING 1971

The Custom-style split diamond on the headstock.

GIBSON
LES PAUL
RECORDING 1973

The complex controls on the Recording.

Jimmy Page performing with Led Zeppelin at Earl's Court, London, in May 1975. He is playing Number One, whose bridge pickup had already been changed from a double-white PAF to a chrome-covered T-Top.

Meanwhile, 1969 was the year of a true sonic revolution that would go on to define the ultimate Les Paul sound. In 1966, Jimmy Page joined the Yardbirds, first as a substitute bass player, then as a dueling lead guitarist along with Jeff Beck, and finally as the sole guitar player. The rest of the band were tired of touring, so Page hired Robert Plant as a singer, who recommended John Bonham from a band they had together, and finally bass player John Paul Jones came to complete the picture. Jones had done a lot of session work alongside Page, so they knew each other well, and they each understood what the other was musically capable of. This dream team started touring in 1968 under the name The New Yardbirds, before settling on the name Led Zeppelin. They didn't waste any time and released their first eponymous album in January 1969.

When he joined the Yardbirds, Page used a Telecaster, which was also the guitar of choice for Clapton and Beck in that band. His 1959 rosewood-fretboard Tele was actually a gift from Beck. It started off as a blonde model, then Page put mirrors on it, before stripping it down and adding a dragon decal. The Dragon Tele was the sound of the first album, that shrill, urgent and biting rock tone that defined a proto-punk riff like "Communication Breakdown".

But the Tele combined with extremely loud Marshall stacks on stage was prone to uncontrollable feedback, and Page was looking for another workhorse. Enter Joe Walsh, who was the guitar player for the Cleveland rock band James Gang and was already hip to the glory of the Burst. James Gang opened for Led Zeppelin on a few US dates, and Walsh gave one his Bursts to Page (*see* page 129).

Unbeknownst to him, Walsh had just unleashed a monster. Page's encounter with the Burst is a lot like the Excalibur tale: a worthy hero finds the ultimate sword and happens to be the only one able to use it to its full extent, in all its noisy glory. *Led Zeppelin II* came out in October 1969, and the magical Burst had done its thing: that second album is miles ahead of the first outing, it is an undeniable hard rock masterpiece by a band firing on all cylinders, fueled by fat riffs that couldn't possibly come out of another guitar:

**GIBSON
CUSTOM SHOP**
JIMMY PAGE
"NUMBER ONE"
LES PAUL

"There's no guarantee that I would have played the... I don't know, it's hypothetical, but I may not have come up with the riff of "Whole Lotta Love" on the Telecaster. That fat sound you're working with, you are inspired – well, I am and I know other people are – by instruments, the sound of the instruments. And then they're playing something they haven't played before – and it's really user-friendly, and suddenly they've got some sort of riff, which is peculiar to that moment. I'm not saying that's the first thing I played on it, but it was to come."

"Whole Lotta Love" is the opening track and one of the most famous songs by Led Zeppelin, but it's the opening track of the B-Side of the LP, "Heartbreaker", that really created the template for all seventies rock to come. The sound is explosive and gritty, the riff is sexy and full of swagger, and at the two-minute point, Page's guitar takes center stage. For the next 50 seconds, the Burst is alone, and Page delivers a glorious solo, brilliantly sloppy, blisteringly fast and full of dynamic nuances. This was unheard of at the time, and instantly became a rite of passage for any player who thought they were worth their salt.

That Burst, nicknamed "Number One", has remained Page's favorite for most of his career. The neck and back of the headstock had been sanded down and shaved before Page got it, so the neck is really thin and there is no serial number, which makes it impossible to know whether

GIBSON CUSTOM SHOP

JIMMY PAGE "NUMBER TWO" LES PAUL

it is a 1959 or 1960 model. Page has swapped the original tuners for gold Grovers, which he already had on his black Custom, and the pickups have been changed a few times. In 1972, the original bridge pickup died, so it was replaced with a T-Top, which was the standard humbucker for Gibson at the time. Then in the nineties he replaced it with a Seymour Duncan, and also replaced the neck pickup with another PAF, probably a better-sounding one. This is especially interesting since most guitar nerds will look down their nose at any humbucker that's not an actual vintage PAF, but most of them are looking for that elusive Zeppelin sound, which Page got by using a lowly T-Top for the bigger part of the band's career. Of course, Page removed the bridge pickup cover to get more treble (and many have imitated him since, sometimes as a straightforward homage), and a push-pull switch has been added to put the two pickups in and out of phase.

In 1973, Page bought a second Burst as a backup, and even though it has been modified to the same specs (shaved-down neck, Grovers, uncovered bridge pickup), that other guitar can be identified thanks to its darker shade of sunburst. Number One was replicated by the Gibson Custom Shop in 2004, Number Two in 2009, Page's black Custom in 2008, and a Jimmy Page signature model was released in 1995. Interestingly, that model and its complex set of controls was the first Les Paul signature model for another player, making it a double signature of sorts. Many more would follow in the years to come.

Amp-wise, Page was pretty secretive about what he was using in the studio, but it eventually transpired that the first album was recorded on a little modded Supro amp. The second album was recorded at various studios while the band was on tour, so it's highly likely that Page plugged in what he found, including a hybrid solid state/ tube Vox UL4120. But the amp that's mostly associated with the Led Zeppelin sound is undoubtedly the Marshall stack. The 100-watt Marshall SLP-1959 (aka "plexi") has become the ultimate head for that rock sound, and since Page used them on stage, that look has become iconic. The combination of a Les Paul with a Marshall stack is the gold standard for a hard rockin' sound, used by thousands of players on countless stages in the wake of Clapton and Page.

PLAY LIST

THE ROLLING STONES
You Can't Always Get What You Want (1969)

KING CRIMSON
21st Century Schizoid Man (1969)

CREEDENCE CLEARWATER REVIVAL
Bad Moon Rising (1969)

LED ZEPPELIN
Heartbreaker (1969)

THE WHO
The Real Me (1973)

SOCIAL DISTORTION
Bad Luck (1992)

HOW JOE WALSH STARTED IT ALL

In 2021, funk guitarist Cory Wong invited Joe Walsh on his podcast, *Wong Notes*. Walsh told the story of the infamous Jimmy Page Number One Les Paul. Most people's idea of the perfect Les Paul sound can be traced back to Led Zeppelin, and Walsh is responsible for a significant part of that sound. "Oddly enough, Jimmy Page played a psychedelic Telecaster in all of The Yardbirds, and the James Gang [Joe's band between 1968 and 1971] opened for Led Zeppelin when they first came to America. We opened for them, and they played four or five places – one of them was Cleveland. And so I met Jimmy, and their first album had just come out [in January 1969], and people were just starting to discover Led Zeppelin. The word of mouth was huge but a lot of people came to hear The Yardbirds songs because that's all they knew. So Jimmy and I became friends because pretty much that's a three-piece band with the lead singer, and Jimmy said to me, 'Look, The Yardbirds is great and I played on so many records...' He played on so many sessions! If you look up what he played on, you'll be amazed. But he said, 'This Telecaster ain't cutting it for Led Zeppelin. And I don't know what to do.' Now, Les Pauls virtually didn't exist in England at the time. They didn't hit popularity yet, and they were pretty easy to find because they hadn't been discovered – and they didn't cost very much.

"After the fact, when that became *the* guitar for rock'n'roll, the rest is history. But he said, 'I got to get a double-coil situation and I've looked for Les Pauls, there aren't any in England. Do you know any way you could

help me get one? Because Led Zeppelin ain't making it with a Telecaster. And I happen to have two. I found one in the basement of a family-owned music store, I think in Athens, Ohio, where Ohio University is. It was just in the basement. I just walked in, and it was all Voxes, and Rickenbackers and Beatles stuff – and I said, 'What do you got downstairs?' And there was a Les Paul! And I found another one through a friend, I traded him some stuff for one. So, one I really liked and one I just was saving for a rainy day, so I gave Jimmy that one, that Les Paul he calls Number One. The body of Led Zeppelin music is that Les Paul that I gave him.

"He'd said, 'I'm in big trouble here.' I said, 'Look, just try this out, I think this will solve the problem. And if you like it, we'll talk.' And several times I thought about asking for it back but that didn't work... He gave me eventually 1,500 bucks or something, and that's less than I paid for it. A little bit less yeah I paid so I broke even on that."

Joe Walsh performing with his band Barnstorm in the early seventies. He is playing a Burst with Grover tuners.

GUERNSEY'S BLACK BEAUTY

On 19th February 2015, one of Les Paul's former guitars was sold through the auction house Guernsey's by Tom Doyle, a close friend of the guitar legend. Even though it is not as historically significant as the auction house made it up to be, it remains a very nice example of how Les Paul would constantly modify his instruments to fit his needs.

The guitar started its life as one of the first Customs in December of 1953, with a Tune-o-matic bridge and a Bigsby vibrato. Just like all of Les Paul's clunkers, it bears a huge black plastic cover between the pickups to hide the extra cavities and modified electronics, like the oversized cavities in the back. The pickups have been changed for low-impedance models with golden surround rings. There's a black knob below the toggle switch and four black chickenhead knobs in a row below the pickguard. The pickguard has been reshaped to accommodate those controls. This unusual Custom even has a microphone input on the upper side of the guitar.

To put it bluntly, this is a late-1953 Custom that has been turned into a much-less desirable Les Paul Personal by Les Paul himself. It sold for $335,000: not too bad for a clunker.

This Custom may be the classiest clunker there has ever been.

THE UNITED STATES OF THE LES PAUL

LOS ANGELES
California

Guns N' Roses started their career in 1985.

FULLERTON
California

Leo Fender started his company in 1946.

DENVER
Colorado

Led Zeppelin played their first US show in 1968.

HOUSTON
Texas

ZZ Top started their career in 1969.

NASHVILLE
Tennessee

The new Gibson factory opened in 1974. Today, it is home to the USA factory, the Custom Shop and the Gibson Garage.

WAUKESHA
Wisconsin

Les Paul was born in 1915.

CHICAGO
Illinois

Mike Bloomfield was born in 1943.

MAHWAH
New Jersey

In 1952, Les Paul bought the mansion where he would spent the rest of his life.

KALAMAZOO
Michigan

The original Gibson factory was located from 1917 to 1984.

BOSTON
Massachussetts

Aerosmith started their career in 1970.

NEW HARTFORD
New York

Joe Bonamassa was born in 1977.

LONG ISLAND CITY
New York

Epiphone guitars were built from 1908 to 1951.

MEMPHIS
Tennessee

The Gibson hollow body factory located from 2001 to 2018.

SOMERSET
Kentucky

Future Gibson CEO Ted McCarty was born in 1909.

I'VE GOT A NEW AXE! IT'S TOO MUCH... IT'S GONNA MAKE ME ROCK ON, MAN!

Steve Marriott opening the first Humble Pie Fillmore East Show
recorded for the 1971 album *Performance: Rockin' The Fillmore*

BIG IN THE SEVENTIES

There's no denying that the seventies were the decade of the Les Paul. It was not only about following in the glorious footsteps of Clapton or Page, but mostly the search for a very specific sound, a thickness and a grit that only a good old Gibson could provide.

Bursts were on virtually every record on the radio, the Custom was becoming the ultimate punk guitar, and for some reason the Les Paul Junior was becoming a viable guitar hero's tool for those who didn't want to play the same gear as everybody else.

At the same time, brand new Les Pauls were coming out of the factory but none of them were exactly the way the players wanted them. The contradiction is obvious: the Les Paul was ubiquitous, but Gibson wasn't invited to that love fest.

TRADING, FINDING AND LOSING

Duane Allman in 1969 with his Gold Top at Muscle Shoals Studios. Note how his strings are going over the stop-bar, not under it.

As the seventies unfolded, more and more pro players turned to the Les Paul to get the fat saturated tones they were looking for. British hard rock pioneers Led Zeppelin, Black Sabbath, Deep Purple, Free and The Who had started the race for louder, bigger and more aggressive tones, and a PAF-equipped Les Paul plugged into a Marshall 1959 SLP could provide exactly that. Guitar equipment was still in its infancy: if you wanted THAT sound, you could only get it from THAT gear. There were no boutique guitar makers building exquisite maple-top solid bodies, no boutique amp makers making hi-end copies of vintage Marshalls, and not a lot of over-drive pedals to get maximum gain and sustain

from your amps. Replacement pickups were not commonplace at all, so you couldn't just stick a humbucker in your Strat and expect it to sound big. In the 1970s Gibson was building Les Pauls that didn't have the Burst sound, so players had to seek an original one. And Marshall stacks were the standard because they were loud enough for most venues, reliable enough for touring, and they would get you that grit, even if you some-times needed to push them a little bit by using a booster (like the Dallas Rangemaster or Elec-tro-Harmonix LPB-1) or a preamp (like the built-in preamp from the Echoplex EP-3 tape delay).

American bands were starting to catch up and one of the most important US bands of the late-sixties is none other than The Allman Brothers, featuring the superhuman slide work of guitarist Duane Allman. Duane got his first Les Paul, a 1957 PAF-equipped Gold Top, in 1969, at the same time that he started the band, as he wrote in a letter to his friend Holly Barr: "Dearest Polly, I got a Les Paul of my very own... Gregg's here gigging with me and I got about the greatest band I ever did hear together and a Marshall amp and two drummers and I quit taking speed and I have been going swimming nekkid in the creek... The name of the band is the Allman Bros..."

Duane Allman playing his first 1959 Burst (his brother Gregg can be seen playing keys in the background).

DEREK AND THE DOMINOS
LAYLA AND OTHER ASSORTED LOVE SONGS
1970

Apart from the not taking speed and swimming naked part, this letter is especially telling of the Holy Grail aspect of a Les Paul and a Marshall amp, even back in 1969. This is the foundation of Allman's tone, and nobody made it sing like he did. He used this Gold Top on the first two albums of his band, and also on the 1970 album *Layla And Other Assorted Love Songs* by Derek and the Dominos, Eric Clapton's band at the time. Clapton was a fan of Allman's playing, Allman had been greatly influenced by Clapton, and both their albums were produced by Tom Dowd so they met, and their deep connection was instantaneous. Clapton, not one to hog the spotlight, then invited Allman to add slide parts to his upcoming album.

A few days later, Duane Allman traded his Gold Top for a 1959 Burst. He had to add a Marshall amp plus $200, which proves that even at that point the price difference between a Gold Top and a Burst was growing. The band's other guitarist, Dickey Betts, was also a Les Paul player, and he had a 1957 Gold Top nicknamed "Goldie", which produced a clearer tone than Duane's thanks to the fact that Dickey was using 100-watt Marshall heads whereas Duane preferred 50 watters that would distort earlier.

Anxious to keep his precious sound but still wanting to taste that Burst sweetness, Allman kept the pickups from his former Gold Top and put them in his new Burst. This is the Burst on the classic 1971 live album *At Fillmore East*, showcasing the band at its very best. Then, he bought another Burst, with a darker more intense color ("darkburst" as collectors call it), but unfortunately did not get to use it much since he died in a bike crash a few months later,

aged 24. Incidentally, the collector who had sold the darkburst to Duane, Kurt Linhof, had been recommended by the singer and guitarist from a little Texas band that was opening for the Allman Brothers, and that man was a perfectly capable Burst player himself. Billy Gibbons of ZZ Top has told the story of his legendary Burst many times, so much so that it has become part of guitar folklore. It goes something like this: Gibbons wanted a Burst because of Clapton. In 1967, as his trio ZZ Top was getting started, he lended a collectively-owned old car to a friend who wanted to become an actress in Hollywood. She used it to drive from Houston to Los Angeles and ended up getting the part she was auditioning for, all thanks to a beat-up car that got nicknamed Pearly Gates since it was the providential tool that helped his friend get where she needed to be. The friend ended up selling the car and she sent part of the money to Gibbons. That same day, Gibbons was going to meet a rancher out of town who had played in a country band and wanted to sell his guitar. The rancher pulled the case from under a bed, and Gibbons bought the 1959 Les Paul for $250, which was exactly the sum sent by his friend that same day. This is how the guitar also got the nickname "Pearly Gates", and this is the Les Paul used by Gibbons to this

GIBSON CUSTOM SHOP
DUANE ALLMAN '59 LES PAUL

Billy Gibbons on stage with ZZ Top in Chicago, 1980.

ALLMAN BROTHERS BAND
AT FILLMORE EAST
1971

PETER FRAMPTON
FRAMPTON COMES ALIVE!
1976

humbuckers. Frampton instantly fell in love with the guitar, and this is the one that he used for the two groundbreaking live albums he has been a part of: Humble Pie's 1971 *Performance: Rockin' The Fillmore* (an absolute masterpiece guitar-heavy album) and his own *Frampton Comes Alive!* (1976), one of the best-selling live albums in music history with more than 11 million copies sold to this day. This album turned Frampton into an idol and his black Custom into the star of the gatefold vinyl cover.

day. He even used it for every ZZ Top concert until the early eighties, at which point he realized that the guitar had become too valuable to travel, especially since he couldn't find another that sounded as good.

"I've spent plenty of money putting together a collection of guitars attempting to find something to replicate Pearly, and it just hasn't happened yet. That's what led to this closet full of hardwood that I have." It's also safe to say that many other players have been buying Les Pauls hoping to get Gibbons' tone, but so far no one has succeeded.

Pearly Gates was replicated by the Gibson Custom Shop back in 2009, which makes it the first limited-edition replica of an artist-owned Burst.

Another legendary Les Paul from that era that has been replicated is The Phenix, Peter Frampton's favorite Custom which has been through hell and back. Peter Frampton was the lead guitarist in the UK band Humble Pie, along with guitarist/singer Steve Marriott. Marriott, formerly of the Small Faces, was a Les Paul enthusiast himself, and he would often play a Gibson-made Dwight guitar, a rebranded version of the Epiphone Coronet (itself the Epiphone version of the double-cut Les Paul Junior). In 1970, Humble Pie were playing at the Fillmore West in San Francisco, and Frampton had just traded his 1962 SG-shaped Les Paul for an ES-335. With the volume that the band was playing at, the 335 wouldn't stop feedbacking, which made the gig a nightmare for Frampton. At the end of it, a friend of his offered to lend him his guitar, a 1954 Les Paul Custom Black Beauty retrofitted with three double-white

Sadly, in 1980, during a tour in South America, the plane that transported the band's gear crashed in Venezuela, and the fire that ensued destroyed most of Frampton's prized possessions. Frampton never really got over losing his Les Paul, so he switched to other types of guitars. Then, in 2001, Gibson made a signature model for him, a beautiful Custom with three double whites based on pictures of his old faithful. But ten years later, in 2011, he got an email from a luthier who had spotted the original in Venezuela. Turns out someone had stolen the instruments from the wreckage, and sold them soon after. The buyer wanted to learn the guitar but didn't pursue it, and when his son tried to learn how to play he decided to have the family Les Paul properly set up. He took it to a luthier who immediately recognized the instrument. A year and a half later, Frampton was finally reunited with his instrument, which was in a sorry state yet still playable. Risen from the ashes, hence the nickname "Phenix".

Peter Frampton performs with his Custom in the late seventies.

Joe Perry on stage with Aerosmith. He is playing his dark Burst 1959 through a talk box, hence the plastic pipe.

MONSTERS OF TONE

A complete list of all the players who got into the Les Paul during the seventies would be a book of its own, and it would be virtually impossible to track down all of the guitarists who recorded an album or three with a Custom, a Junior or even a Burst. As YouTuber and Les Paul enthusiast Rick Beato puts it: "In the seventies, every guitarist either played a Les Paul or a Strat, and a lot of them actually played both." It was the de facto Excalibur for most rock-influenced guitar heroes of the era, in a way that had never happened before, and that hasn't happened since: in the fifties and sixties, the Les Paul was biding its time, and many players would gravitate towards the simpler charms of Fender guitars. But they were not ubiquitous and other options were still popular, like archtops in the fifties and Rickenbacker or Gretsch guitars in the sixties. It seems as though by the end of the sixties, most of them had become aware of the magic that could be created with a humbucker and a Marshall stack. Therefore, it is safe to say that a very significant portion of all albums recorded between 1969 and 1979 owe part of their sonic personality to Lester's guitar.

Among the most influential guitar players of the era, Carlos Santana was one of the greats who got their "real" start at the 1969 Woodstock festival, especially with the 1970 movie that heavily showcased his legendary performance of "Soul Sacrifice" with an SG Special. The band Santana's self-titled debut album came out a few weeks after the Woodstock performance, and starting with their third album, *Santana III* (1971), the guitarist switched to a Les Paul, a 1968 Custom sunburst reissue. Since that color wasn't readily available, it was probably a black custom that had been refinished. Following a deal with

Gibson, he switched over to the strange Gibson L-6S in 1974, but those precious few years with the Custom showcase Carlos Santana at his juiciest, warmest and most-intense sounding.

Back in Great Britain, progressive rock was all the rage and some daring, intense guitar parts were being recorded using a Les Paul. Steve Hackett of Genesis bought a 1957 Gold Top in 1972, which he used from the *Selling England By The Pound* album onwards. Just like most players of the era, Hackett's lust for a Les Paul came from one of the usual suspects: "I heard Peter Green playing a Les Paul live with John Mayall in 1966. I loved the sound and always searched for it."

In 1973, three debut albums were released by bands that did their part to make the Les Paul inescapable. *Pronounced 'Lĕh-'nérd 'Skin-'nérd* was the first album by Florida band Lynyrd Skynyrd. They came in the wake of the Southern Rock success of the Allman Brothers, which had taught them how good two contrasting Gibsons could sound. Allen Collins had an SG and a Firebird, while Gary Rossington had a 1959 Burst. And even though Ed King was the bass player in the band, he was a great guitarist in his own right and also owned a 1959 Burst. His was nicknamed "Redeye" because of the distinctive

LYNYRD SKYNYRD
(PRONOUNCED 'LĔH-'NÉRD 'SKIN-'NÉRD)
1973

GENESIS
SELLING ENGLAND BY THE POUND
1973

GIBSON
CUSTOM GARY ROSSINGTON '59 LES PAUL STANDARD

patch of red aniline dye between the neck pickup and the toggle switch. This was the feature that allowed him to recognize it and track it down after it was stolen from him.

Montrose's first album was self-titled, and it featured singer Sammy Hagar as well as the namesake of the band, guitarist Ronnie Montrose. He had a 1958 Burst that ended up getting stolen (yes, that one too – concert security was basically nonexistent at the time). Montrose was quite open about where his idea of playing a Les Paul came from: "I'd seen Eric Clapton, Jeff Beck and Duane Allman all playing Sunbursts."

GIBSON
LES PAUL CUSTOM
SUNBURST 1973

Another self-titled debut released in 1973 made a lot of future players aware of the power and might of the Les Paul. *Aerosmith* by Aerosmith was chock-full of great songs, from "Mama Kin" to "Dream On". Both guitarists, Joe Perry and Brad Whitford, were using Les Pauls, and they both have collected a considerable amount of vintage Bursts, Gold Tops and Customs over the years.

Shock-rock demigods Kiss were also playing Les Pauls starting with their 1974 debut album, and singer/guitarist Paul Stanley has had his fair share of Bursts in his collection. Lead guitarist Ace Frehley was famous for his three-pickup Les Pauls without covers. The neck pickup on his black Custom was a dummy that would hide a little device, part of Kiss' famous on-stage theatrics: "There's an asbestos-covered metal box under the rhythm pickup…a battery pack that jettisons the smoke bomb and a halogen lamp to make the guitar look like it's on fire - though it *does* catch fire half the time. I never used my rhythm pickup anyway, so I converted its volume and tone knobs to trigger the smoke and light." That highly toxic display of pyrotechnics was used every night for Frehley's solo spot, and it eventually earned him one of the first Les Paul signature models in 1997, plus a signature Les Paul Custom in 2011 and a gorgeous '59 Burst reissue in 2015, even though by then he had been out of the band for over a decade.

In 1975, Fleetwood Mac changed its sound completely. The British band that used to be Peter Green's outfit turned half-American when they welcomed singer Stevie Nicks and guitarist/singer Lindsey Buckingham. These two brought a renewed energy to the unit, which resulted in two best-selling albums in a row, the second eponymous album (1975) and the record-breaking *Rumours* (1977 – over 40 million copies sold). Buckingham was mostly playing Fenders before joining the band, but he switched over to a 1974 white Les Paul Custom that he would fingerpick for a very special sound. "The band wanted me to play a humbucker guitar because Mick Fleetwood tuned his drums fairly low and Christine McVie's keyboard sounds were kind of Wurlitzer-like and Rhodes-y. All that lower-midrange stuff tended to make the Telecaster really scratchy and thin."

Also in 1975, another band changed its sound by welcoming a new guitarist to the fold, namely Eagles with Joe Walsh on board. The former James Gang guitar player had already started his solo career but he joined the California band that was at the peak of its powers at the time. The resulting album, *Hotel California* (1976), has become an all-time classic, and its timeless title track features a dueling solo by Don Felder and Joe Walsh. Even though Walsh had owned several Bursts and was often using a 1960 Standard (replicated in 2013), he picked a Tele for that solo since Felder was already playing a '59 Burst (replicated in 2010).

In 1977, Cheap Trick released their eponymous debut album, featuring the juicy-sounding riffs of Rick Nielsen, who was one of the earliest collectors of vintage guitars. As such, he has owned and used many Bursts, including a '59 that was replicated in 2017. But in the late seventies, Nielsen was also heavily relying on Hamer guitars. These were built in a small Illinois workshop (near Cheap Trick's hometown of Rockford), made with the same quality and attention to details as older Les Pauls. They were good enough for a true vintage enthusiast like Nielsen, and a sign of more trouble to come on the Gibson front.

CHEAP TRICK
CHEAP TRICK
1977

Carlos Santana on stage in 1971 with his sunburst Custom.

PRIZED POSSESSION

In 2018, when Ed King of Lynyrd Skynyrd passed, his widow got in touch with the Nashville store Carter Vintage Guitars in order to sell his most significant instrument, including the 1973 Stratocaster he used to record "Sweet Home Alabama" and his beloved 1959 Burst nicknamed "Red Eye" after the patch of red aniline below the toggle switch.

In order to demo some of those guitars, Walter Carter, the owner of the store, called Jason Isbell, four-time Grammy winning singer/songwriter and bona fide guitar geek. Jason made the video demos on a brownface Fender amp, and fell madly in love with the Burst.

"I picked it up and I got lost on the way home that day. I couldn't sleep, and I just couldn't stop thinking about this guitar. So I called my accountant and she said, 'No, that's ridiculous, you can't have that guitar'. So I called my manager, and I told her I need you to find me a bunch of weird birthday parties to play this year. No terrible people, just find me some crazy wild private gigs 'cause I've got to buy this guitar. And so I got this guitar!"

After changing the tuners and the stopbar, Red Eye was ready to become Isbell's favorite guitar, one that he uses in the studio and even on stage: "The middle position on this is very, very special, even for a 1959 Les Paul... The neck profile is perfect... It's my prized possession... I try not to drop it, but other than that I'm gonna use it... I think it's supposed to be played."

JUNIOR HAS GROWN UP

The seventies were a time of appreciation for the lowly Les Paul Junior. It seems like a lot of players who were more interested in sound than looks tended to gravitate towards Gibson's budget P90 monster. It seems like that redemption can find its very precise origin in a show that took place in Bethel, New York on Saturday 16th August, 1969. The four-piece band Mountain from Long Island had been playing on the East Coast for a while when they arrived at Max Yasgur's farm for the second day of the Woodstock Festival. They took to the stage at 9p.m. after Canned Heat (featuring Alan Wilson and a gorgeous 1954 wraparound Gold Top), and proceeded to blow everyone's mind. Mountain was not a household name to say the least: in fact they didn't even have an album out at that time. Guitarist and singer Leslie West had released a solo album a few weeks prior called *Mountain* produced by Felix Pappalardi, who became the bass player and second singer in Mountain. Pappalardi was also the man who produced *Disraeli Gears* in 1967, probably the studio pinnacle for Clapton's trio Cream, and that connection should not be overlooked: Mountain was an evolution of Cream, the American answer to that groundbreaking and self-indulgent British power trio, with the very same fiery passion and freedom.

And like Clapton in Cream, Leslie West played a Les Paul... Except his was a Junior. This was Pappalardi's idea: he gave his Junior to West because he thought he would sound good with it. And he did. The story makes sense since Pappalardi was a producer, so he had an ear for what guitars sounded best, regardless of fashion or what they looked like. He's the first who heard the dynamic bite of the Junior and thought it was great, even though it was not a sophisticated instrument at all. Like West said: "It reminded me of a tree with a microphone. It stuck."

Visually, the Junior was a strange choice for Leslie West. He truly was a mountain of a man, and in his hands the single-cut sunburst mid-fifties Junior looked like a toy. But it sounded like an earthquake and lava flowing at the same time. In just a few minutes, West proved that he was the most badass player at a festival that also included Santana, Alvin Lee with Ten Years After and Johnny Winter. The world took note, and musicians especially took note. Many guitarists trace their Junior fascination back to Leslie West, and at that time they were cheap enough that they could be bought just to see what all the fuss was about. Rick Nielsen (Cheap Trick), who was already collecting them at that point, said: "I've always liked them. They're so cool, and they were so cheap originally. 150, 120, 100, maybe 175 tops (*in dollars*). I've probably had 50. Juniors were always an easy trade... you throw in a couple of these guys and the money adds up on the debtor or the credit side. But I always liked 'em, and they were always the coolest ones... I always liked the TV Yellow ones. I prefer the double cut one, cause you can get higher on the neck."

GIBSON CUSTOM SHOP "INSPIRED BY" JOHN LENNON LES PAUL JUNIOR

MOUNTAIN
CLIMBING!
1970

YES
TALES FROM
TOPOGRAPHIC
OCEANS
1973

The British rock band Mott The Hoople had toured with Mountain, and guitarist Mick Ralphs, who had used an SG/Les Paul on the band's debut album, switched to a Junior under West's influence: "Even though it had one pickup, it was real ballsy. I loved it because it was like a hunk of wood with two knobs on it. I found one for about $100 in a junk store. I used that guitar constantly for the rest of Mott the Hoople, usually through a 100w Marshall amp."

Martin Barre from British progressive rock icons Jethro Tull was playing his through a Hiwatt amp, an even more deafening proposition. In fact the whole of their classic best-selling 1971 album *Aqualung* was recorded with only a 1958 single-cutaway Junior. "We'd played in America with a band called Mountain, and I loved Leslie West's sound. I thought his tone was tremendous, so I bought a Les Paul Junior. That was the only guitar I used on the *Aqualung* album." Judging from the beautiful runaway feedback at the beginning of his solo on "Aqualung", it's safe to imagine that Barre was really cranking up his Hiwatt. He then switched over to a gorgeous 1958 Burst, but his sound was never that edgy again.

Steve Howe from Yes was also a notorious collector and he would use one guitar per album to keep a coherent sound throughout. And for their monster 1973 double album *Tales From Topographic Oceans*, that guitar was a 1955 single-cutaway sunburst Junior. "Generally it had a sound: you plug it in, and there it is...the Junior is on most of sides two, three, and four, where it's the key guitar. Side four in particular is all about the Junior." It's particularly interesting that a man as passionate about beautiful guitars as Steve Howe (who owns many Gibson electric archtops) would use a Junior for such an ambitious and grandiose project as that double album. But as Steve said, the Junior has one sound, and when you're already dealing with convoluted musical structures and complex arrangements, it feels good to know that you don't have to worry about what your guitar sound should be.

Another little Junior that went on to achieve greatness belonged to John Lennon. He didn't perform a lot on stage after the Beatles' breakup, and would concentrate on studio work in his new hometown of New York. In 1972, however, he played the Madison Square Garden for a charity, and appeared in an Army jacket holding a cherry-red single-cutaway Junior, modded with a Tune-o-matic bridge and a Charlie Christian neck pickup. Visions of rock stardom don't come any cooler than that.

Another absolute icon who enjoyed the simplicity of a mahogany plank with two pickups on it was Bob Marley. From his first worldwide success in 1973 until his untimely death in 1981, he almost exclusively played a heavily-modified fifties single-cutaway Special, stripped to a brownish hue with a headstock binding and rectangle neck inlays. That iconic instrument was replicated by the Gibson Custom Shop in 2002, and Lennon's was replicated in 2007. Those replicas were objects of workmanship for hardcore fans only, since at that time you could find a modified fifties Junior or Special for about the same price as those limited-edition replicas.

John Lennon on stage on 30 August 1973 at Madison Square Garden (New York City)

Leslie West in the zone with a single-cut Les Paul Junior

DOUBLE-CUT FREAKS

NEW YORK DOLLS
TOO MUCH TOO
SOON
1974

RIGHT Johnny
Thunders on stage in
1989, still rocking the
double-cut.

OPPOSITE Keith
Richards with the
Rolling Stones on
stage in London,
2012. He is playing the
"Dice" Les Paul Junior.

The double-cutaway Junior was not as popular, probably due to Leslie West's influence and maybe also because the single-cutaway Junior had the "proper" Les Paul shape, which must have helped to make it more desirable. Two renegades have flown the double-cut flag, and they may very well be the most important Junior heroes. The first one was Keith Richards. Yes, him again: the Rolling Stones man has used many different guitars over the course of a very long career. The Junior first entered his collection in 1972, when the band was recording *Goat's Head Soup* in Kingston, Jamaica. Keith really connected with that 1960 Cherry Red double-cutaway Junior, to the point that it became his main instrument for 1973 and 1974.

In 1979, for his side-project The New Barbarians, Richards picked up a bunch of new guitars, including a 1957 single-cutaway sunburst Junior, and a 1958 double-cutaway TV Yellow Junior nicknamed Dice after the dice decal that he put on the front. Just like on his Cherry-Red 1960, he replaced the original wraparound bridge with an adjustable Badass, and he put new Grover tuners on it. Those mods were very commonplace at the time for any pro player who wanted to use their Junior to its full extent, to get a guitar that played in tune and stayed in tune. Gibsons have come and gone as part of the Stones' arsenal since then, but Dice is still around, and it has seen more use than most other instruments in Keith's arsenal. It has been closely associated with him since they make a perfect pair: the Junior no-nonsense vibe absolutely matches Keith's pre-punk swagger and nonchalance.

Speaking of punk, the other absolute double-cutaway TV Yellow hero is Johnny Thunders. He used to be the other guitar player in the defining pre-punk outfit New York Dolls, along with Sylvain Sylvain who was also keen on Juniors. On the cover of their second album, *Too Much Too Soon* (1974), Sylvain has a Black Beauty and Thunders has a TV Special. Then, in 1975, Thunders launched his own band, the Heartbreakers (not to be confused with Tom Petty's band of the same name), and toured with them until they disbanded in 1978, after having released the seminal album *L.A.M.F.* (1977). By then, Johnny Thunders had picked up a double-cutaway TV Junior, a rare version with the tortoise pickguard instead of the usual black one, which he customized with stickers. Once again, that guitar was perfectly fitting for the unusual character that was Thunders: bare-bones, unsophisticated but undeniably special.

Mick Ronson on stage with Bowie for the final show of the Ziggy Stardust Tour, on 3rd July 1973 at the Hammersmith Odeon, London.

GLAMOROUS PUNKS

The New York Dolls and Thunders' attitude in particular were deeply influential for the burgeoning British punk scene. In the US, they were mostly notorious in New York City for their outrageous shows, but in the UK they were bona fide superstars. Thunders is the whole reason why Mick Jones from The Clash picked up a double-cutaway Junior (many of them, in fact). And rumor has it that fashion designer Malcolm McLaren saw the Dolls play in New York and that's how he got the idea of putting the Sex Pistols together. And it is indeed pretty obvious that Steve Jones' stage moves can be traced back to Thunders' attitude.

But Jones didn't play a Junior. He played a Custom. A 1974 white Custom with the pickguard and pickup covers removed, and with stickers of course. So how do you stay faithful to the proletarian punk ethos while playing such a luxurious bourgeois instrument? Tell the journalists you stole it, of course!

But that Custom is a very telling symbol of the essence of the Sex Pistols. For all of the attitude and posing, deep down they were just kids who absolutely loved glam rock and wanted to do their version of it while looking tough and not wearing a boa. The Pistols' album *Never Mind The Bollocks, Here's the Sex Pistols* (1977) sounded like a T-Rex influenced wall of sound with a snotty singer.

Mick Ronson was David Bowie's guitarist from 1970 to 1973, culminating with the classic *The Rise and Fall Of Ziggy Stardust and the Spiders From Mars* in 1972. He was the perfect counterpart to Bowie, a sexy blond adonis, a fierce riffmeister with a harsh pointy sound, but

also a very capable piano player, even going as far as writing the string arrangements for the whole album. His no-frills rocking approach to sound and playing was a huge influence on the punk generation, and so was his use of a 1968 early reissue Les Paul Custom with the black finish sanded-down to the natural maple, with the pickup covers removed, plugged into a Tone Bender mkI and a monstrous 200-watt Marshall Major head.

While Ronson was the moody silent sidekick, Marc Bolan was the undeniable frontman of T-Rex, the singer, the guitar player, the songwriter, the founder of the band and the eternal poster boy for early-seventies glam rock. He was seen with several guitars, including a white Strat and a Flying V, but the guitar Bolan remains closely associated with was a Burst that Bolan had sanded off and then refinished to a transparent orange color as a tribute to the orange Gretsch of his idol, Eddie Cochran. Bolan broke the neck on this Standard, so it was replaced with a Custom neck, hence the weird hybrid appearance that made it fully his, complete with a zebra pickup at the neck and a black one at the bridge. Bolan can be seen in a classic rock'n'roll pose on the cover of his classic 1971 album *Electric Warrior*, playing his Les Paul in front of a roaring Vampower stack (a British solid state brand that did not become a classic). That guitar was replicated by the Gibson Custom Shop in 2011 in its last version with the Custom-neck and "Bolan-Chablis" finish.

One last proto-punk player worth mentioning is James Williamson. In 1970, Detroit's The Stooges were falling apart, and a few months after Williamson joined as a second guitarist, the

DAVID BOWIE
THE RISE AND FALL OF ZIGGY STARDUST AND THE SPIDERS FROM MARS
1972

IGGY AND THE STOOGES
RAW POWER
1973

SEX PISTOLS
NEVER MIND THE BOLLOCKS, HERE'S THE SEX PISTOLS
1977

band split up. In 1972, Iggy Pop and Williamson got the band back together, this time with Ron Asheton on bass instead of guitar. With that line-up, the Stooges recorded the seminal 1973 album *Raw Power*, produced by David Bowie. Williamson's sound and playing are fierce and savage as can be, and created the blueprint for the shape of punk to come. His main weapon was a 1969 Les Paul Custom with a pancake body and a very red Cherry Sunburst finish not unlike the color on the Deluxes of the era. A strange choice, but Williamson made it work so brilliantly that no one would even dare questioning it.

On the opposite side of the spectrum, Al Di Meola joined pianist Chick Corea's band Return to Forever in 1971 at the age of nineteen while he was still studying at Berklee. That band was at the forefront of jazz/rock fusion: Corea had played in Miles Davis' historic albums *In A Silent Way* (1969) and *Bitches Brew* (1970), while Di Meola was playing a brand-new 1971 black Les Paul Custom on dimed Marshall stacks. The mixture was unexpected, but it worked to very good effect and Return To Forever enjoyed a great amount of both critical and commercial success in the seventies. That Custom is also on the cover of Di Meola's second solo album, *Elegant Gypsy* (1977), which features the lightning-fast "Race With Devil On Spanish Highway".

In 1972, Di Meola met Larry DiMarzio, who was starting his company. DiMarzio developed custom-made double-white humbucking pickups for Di Meola's Custom, which considerably helped DiMarzio's business get off the ground, and Di Meola also bought DiMarzio's 1958 Les Paul Standard. Di Meola preferred black guitars, so he had Gibson refinish it in the eighties, a refinish operation which they probably would refuse to perform today, since it would considerably harm the value of such a highly collectible instrument.

T REX
ELECTRIC WARRIOR
1971

AL DI MEOLA
ELEGANT GYPSY
1977

GIBSON CUSTOM SHOP
MARC BOLAN SIGNATURE LES PAUL

The last concert by the original Sex Pistols, 14th January 1978 in San Francisco. From left to right: Johnny Rotten and Steve Jones.

Marc Bolan playing his Les Paul in front of the same Vampower stack that can be seen on the cover of *Electric Warrior*. At the time, the Les Paul didn't have the first-fret inlay Custom neck yet.

PLAY LIST

MOUNTAIN
Mississippi Queen (1970)

ALLMAN BROTHERS BAND
Statesboro Blues (live)
(1971)

HUMBLE PIE
Four Day Creep (live) (1971)

SANTANA
Everybody's Everything
(1971)

T. REX
Jeepster (1971)

JETHRO TULL
Aqualung (1971)

DAVID BOWIE
Suffragette City (1972)

MOTT THE HOOPLE
All The Young Dudes (1972)

GENESIS
Firth Of Fifth (1973)

YES
Ritual (Nous Sommes
du Soleil) (1973)

THE ROLLING STONES
Dancing With Mr D. (1973)

THE STOOGES
Search and Destroy (1973)

LYNYRD SKYNYRD
Free Bird (1973)

AEROSMITH
Mama Kin (1973)

MONTROSE
Bad Motor Scooter (1973)

KISS
Deuce (1974)

EAGLES
Life In The Fast Lane (1976)

FLEETWOOD MAC
The Chain (1977)

**JOHNNY THUNDERS & THE
HEARTBREAKERS**
Born Too Loose (1977)

THE SEX PISTOLS
Pretty Vacant (1977)

CHEAP TRICK
I Want You To Want Me
(1977)

AL DI MEOLA
Race with Devil on Spanish
Highway (1977)

THE 10 MOST EXPENSIVE LES PAULS

It should be no surprise by now: vintage Les Pauls are among the most expensive guitars out there. At the time of writing, several Bursts were on sale for more than $300,000, and in the mid-noughties they could sometimes be sold for half a million. But some of them would be likely to command even higher prices of they ever came up for sale, and a few Les Pauls have already made headlines by being sold for historic sums at auction. This top 10 is in two parts: first, four Les Pauls that would command eye-watering sums if they ever came up for sale, followed by six Les Pauls that have actually sold at auction.

1 - THE BEANO BURST

ESTIMATE: $20 million

As the one that started it all, this is probably the one that would sell for the heftiest sum. Clapton only owned it for a year from 1965 to 1966, then it was stolen, never to be seen again, which only added to the mystery and mystique surrounding it. If it were to resurface, the guitar would need to be properly authenticated based on the wood patterns in the maple top, since nobody knows its serial number, and Clapton doesn't remember whether it was a '59 or a '60. All we know is how good it sounded on *John Mayall and the Bluesbreakers with Eric Clapton*, and the fact that it turned everybody else on to the magic of the Burst.

2 - JIMMY PAGE NUMBER ONE

ESTIMATE: $15 million

Even though it has been modded, this is probably the most expensive Burst whose whereabouts are known. Page is one of the most important artists ever to have played a Les Paul, and by Led Zeppelin's second album in 1969, he had defined how the famous Gibson model was supposed to sound. And it was all done on that Burst sold to Jimmy by Joe Walsh. This is the magic one, Excalibur, the one that has always been by the wizard's side.

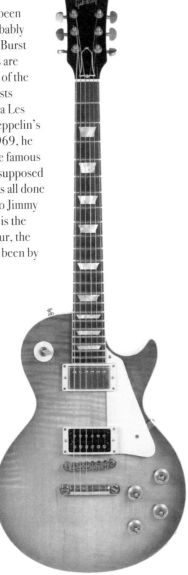

3 - PEARLY GATES

ESTIMATE: $10 million

Pearly Gates is among the guitars that started the obsession for the 1959 Les Paul, a Burst that turned the Burst into an object of desire. Billy Gibbons purchased it in 1969 when he was starting ZZ Top, and the guitar became the sound of the band, the sound of Texas blues and the ultimate fat juicy sound of a humbucker-equipped Les Paul. Pearly Gates herself is almost as famous as her owner, and it became the first guitar that was properly replicated by the Gibson Custom Shop.

4 - GREENY

ESTIMATE: $5 million

Back when Kirk Hammett bought the 1959 Les Paul formerly owned by Peter Green and Gary Moore, rumor had it that he had bought it for something like two million dollars, which sounds about right given the legendary status accorded to it by its previous rockstar owners. According to the Metallica soloist himself, the collector who sold Greeny to him needed cash fast so he got it at a much lower price. But if it came up for sale now, the added bonus of having toured and recorded with Metallica would probably help send it through the financial roof.

10 MOST EXPENSIVE LES PAULS

5 - DUANE ALLMAN'S 1957 GOLD TOP

SOLD for $1.25 million in 2019

Surprisingly, the Les Paul that sold for the highest price at auction wasn't a Burst: it was Duane Allman's 1957 humbucker-equipped Gold Top. This guitar doesn't have its original pickups any more and it has been refinished twice, yet it became a million-dollar instrument, which gives an idea of Allman's renown in the guitar world. This is the Les Paul used for the first two Allman Brothers Band albums and Eric Clapton's Derek And The Dominos album, *Layla And Other Assorted Love Songs*.

6 - LES PAUL'S 1952 GOLD TOP "NUMBER ONE"

SOLD for $930,000 in 2021

That Les Paul belonged to Les Paul himself, and it has been presented as the one Les approved for the model to go into production. As such, it obviously represents a very important moment in guitar history. It is an instrument that has been heavily modified by Les throughout the years, showing a few of the specs he enjoyed: a DeArmond neck pickup, a Kauffman vibrato, chickenhead knobs and hidden phantom coils to buck the hum. An unmistakable tribute to the tinkering genius of Les Paul himself.

7 - DAVID GILMOUR'S 1955 GOLD TOP

SOLD for $447,000 in 2019

The David Gilmour auction in 2019 was a crazy milestone in the guitar collecting world, since many guitars saw their price skyrocket thanks to their association with the Pink Floyd frontman. A three-pickup 1959 Black Beauty sold for $200,000, but one of the most impressive transactions of the auction was this lovely 1955 wraparound Gold Top. Part of the staggering $447,000 that it sold for is down to this guitar having been plugged straight into the mixer to record the final solo on "Another Brick in the Wall (Part 2)", the gloomy single and unlikely disco hit taken from *The Wall* in 1979. Many believe it to be one of the most beautiful Strat sounds ever, yet it is a P90-equipped Les Paul!

10 MOST EXPENSIVE LES PAULS

8 - NEAL SCHON'S 1959 BURST

SOLD for $350,000 in 2021

Neal Schon got his first big-time gig as part of the Santana band in 1971, but he fully realized his personal vision in 1975 when he formed the project Journey. In 2021, he sold a few of his best guitars, including instruments that have been used on classic hits written by Schon, such as the late-seventies Deluxe modded with a Floyd Rose heard on "Don't Stop Believing", which sold for $250,000. This is especially impressive since modded Deluxes usually sell for much less than that. On the other hand, Schon's beautiful 1959 Burst sold for $350,000, which is not that much more than what it would have cost without the Schon association.

9 - LES PAUL'S 1953 CUSTOM

SOLD for $330,000 in 2015

This is the second Les Paul-owned Les Paul that sold for an impressive amount at auction. That Custom had been modified with low-impedance pickups, new controls and a microphone input, yet it was still a sensation in 2015 since this apparently was the first Custom made for Les Paul before it went into production. The guitar was on the cover of *Guitar Player* magazine at the time of the auction, and it probably helped solidify its status as an iconic instrument.

10 - THE EDGE'S WHITE CUSTOM

SOLD for $288,000 in 2007

Music Rising is a charity created by U2's The Edge and producer Bob Ezrin in 2005 to help musicians survive after Hurricane Katrina hit New Orleans. A Music Rising auction took place in 2007 and it featured several U2-owned pieces of memorabilia, including one of The Edge's most important guitars, along with his black Stratocaster and Explorer. The 1975 Custom was a turning point for The Edge's sound, and it is surprising it did not sell for more than $288,000. It still represents a pretty good price for a seventies Custom, but back in 2007 auctioned guitars were not the crazy phenomenon they have become today. If this guitar came under the hammer today, it would probably sell for more.

WHAT'S THE BEST THIS GUITAR EVER WAS? ARE WE BUILDING IT LIKE THAT NOW? AND IF NOT, WHY NOT?

Tim Shaw

The eighties were not easy on Gibson. To be fair, they were not easy on any of the "heritage" guitar brands: Gretsch's owner Baldwin went bankrupt in 1983, Fender was sold by CBS to employees of the company in 1985 (and for a short stint, US production of the brand stopped altogether), and Martin almost went the way of the dinosaur due to a strike in 1982.

Of course, this was also due to acoustic guitars being totally uncool within the new musical landscape. In 1980, the music television channel MTV was launched, which started an era of musicians having to look good rather than play well. British company Simmons started building electronic drum kits that same year. Also that year, the LM-1 Linn Electronics drum machine as well as the Oberheim DMX (also a drum machine) became the new standard for super tight and easy-to-mix drums without having to go through the hassle of hiring a drummer, booking a studio and miking up a drum kit. In 1983, the Yamaha DX-7 synthesizer became the ultimate gizmo that made every record sound polished, slick and modern. Incidentally, this is also the year when the MIDI system was introduced to the world.

The electric guitar was still a force to be reckoned with, but it had to compete with keyboards by becoming sharper and more distorted. The Les Paul looked strangely out of place during that decade, even though it never really left the airwaves.

PLAY YOUR GUITAR ON THE MTV

CLOSE, BUT NO CIGAR

From the mid-seventies on, Gibson had been trying to expand the Les Paul line by adding new versions. But not all variations of the Les Paul can be the Custom, the Junior or even the Deluxe: some of them were downright weird, and they usually did not spend much time in the catalog. Not all of them were bad guitars, but they just couldn't capture the musical zeitgeist or match what musicians expected from the model they knew and loved. Some of these have become collector's items for three good reasons: first, they represent a "parallel universe" kind of approach to collecting Les Pauls, since Gold Tops and Bursts are so commonplace for collectors, those leftfield variations end up having a special appeal. Secondly, these guitars are artifacts of a time gone by, and most of them have not been reissued. They are time capsules, witness to strange times in the guitar market, and most collections have at least a partly historical approach. Finally, Les Pauls from the fifties and even sixties are getting more and more expensive, and later decades are a nice way of scoring an old-wood guitar with a story to tell without going completely broke.

Among those "alternative" Les Pauls of the era, one of the most striking was the Artisan. This over-the-top 1976 contraption had Custom specs (multiple bindings, ebony fretboard, three pickups, maple top, gold hardware), including a three-piece maple neck (which was becoming more and more common at the time), but with really unusual banjo-style neck and headstock inlays, and the old Gibson script logo. It was originally available in walnut only, then other colors appeared, a two-pickup version was made and in 1978 the tailpiece had fine tuners instead of the usual stop bar, just like on a Floyd Rose

Matt Pike from Sleep playing his three-pickup Artisan (modded with Lace Sensor pickups) plugged into Orange stacks.

Dave Davies from The Kinks rocking an Artisan in the seventies.

the bobbins. Those came as a replacement for "patent number" humbuckers used from 1962 to 1965. But the Artisan did not feature the T-Tops of the era, instead it had Series VII pickups with a high output level, probably designed to keep up with spare pickup companies that were coming up with hotter humbuckers at the time. On the three-pickup version, the center humbucker was another model with a lower resistance, called the Super Humbucker.

The 1973 Les Paul Signature was a weird offset Gold Top ES-335 with high-impedance pickups (spoiler alert: it tanked).

The 1975 The Les Paul was a Custom covered in wood: the top, back, side and neck were all violin-grade flamed maple, while the pickguard, pickup rings, poker chip and knobs were made from rosewood. Even the multiple bindings were made of wood. The guitar was so time-consuming to build and its price was so high that it never really got off the ground in a significant way.

1975 also marked the reinvention of a model that has remained central to the Gibson line to this day: the Les Paul Standard. For the first time since 1960, this name was being used for a humbucker-equipped Les Paul-shaped guitar. That was the point when Gibson decided which specs made a Standard, and those rules have remained relatively untouched since then. Of course there have been countless versions and variations of the Standard, including leftfield ideas, but the usual requirements for a Standard have remained for half a century since: two humbuckers, a Tune-o-matic bridge, crown inlays, binding around the top and fretboard, rosewood fretboard, carved maple top, mahogany body and neck. Many, many colors have been available throughout the years, but popular choices have been ebony, white, wine red and any shade of sunburst you can think of.

The new-for-1976 Les Paul Pro Deluxe was a new version of the Deluxe with cream P90s instead of the mini humbuckers, and ebony for the fretboard, while the 1978 The Paul was a new take on the Junior idea of building a budget Les Paul, complete with a walnut satin-finished contoured body, an ebony fingerboard with dot inlays, a decal headstock logo and two exposed

except the Artisan didn't have a vibrato. Those TP-6 tailpieces were an experiment of the time, but they remain standard on B.B. King's Lucille model to this day. The Artisan was the most luxurious Les Paul yet, but it failed to capture the imagination of players, except for British rock royalty Dave Davies (from the Kinks), who played a 1977 model with three pickups, and Matt Pike from stoner kings Sleep who had picked up a very similar version.

The pickups on the Artisan were quite special. At the time, Gibson had switched to T-Top humbuckers, so called because of the T letter that would be seen etched in each of

PLAY YOUR GUITAR ON THE MTV

From left to right
1978 Gibson ad for the Les Paul 25/50.

1974 Gibson ad for the Les Paul Signature.

1982 Gibson ad for the Les Paul 30th Anniversary.

humbuckers. Even though it looked quite plain, the The Paul was actually a pretty well-made guitar for the price and its bare-bones attitude has made it a cheap and easy-to-modify Gibson favorite on the used market.

Finally, there were also a few Anniversary models of the Les Paul made to celebrate birthdays of their flagship guitar. The first one was released in 1974 to commemorate twenty years of the Custom. It was a 1968-style Custom (maple top and two humbuckers) with a "twentieth anniversary" inlay at the fifteen fret, available in black, white and wine red. That first attempt at blowing their candles was a commercial success, which is probably what prompted Gibson to make more.

They did not wait for a full decade, and instead picked both the 25th anniversary of the Les Paul Model in 1977 and the 50th anniversary of Les Paul's career start as a musician and released the 25/50 Anniversary Les Paul in 1978 (close enough!). This gorgeous creation also had 1968 Custom-style appointments with Super 400 split blocks fretboard inlays, fine tuners, two Super VII humbuckers and a Cremona sunburst finish typical of older Gibson archtop guitars and mandolins. In order to commemorate the fact that this was both a silver and a gold anniversary guitar, the hardware was mixed, with chrome

tuner buttons and gold hardware on the body. The Custom Burst met with resounding success.

The Les Paul Artist model, which came out in 1979, was close to that 25/50 Anniversary since it was a maple-topped Custom with gold hardware, fine tuners, an exclusive headstock inlay that read LP, but also a contoured back and a system of active electronics which explained the huge cavities in the back.

Finally, in 1982, the 30th Anniversary Les Paul was much closer to the original Gold Top, except it was the 1957 version with humbuckers and a Tune-o-matic bridge. This era was the start of Gibson offering proper reissues of its past glories, and not only on their birthdays.

165

A LONG WAY

GIBSON
LES PAUL
HERITAGE
STANDARD 1980

Nowadays, we take Burst reissues for granted. There have been dozens of meticulously made exact replicas of 1958–1960 Les Paul Standard, and that version of the Les Paul has been the gold standard for the Custom Shop for decades. Any well-off collector has at least one of these in their guitar room, and we're even lucky enough that we get to pick the year, the exact specs, the precise shade of sunburst, the artificial aging of the guitar, even sometimes the piece of maple that will be used for the top. Back in the seventies, reissuing the Burst did not seem like an obvious decision for Gibson. They had reissued the mid-fifties Gold Top and the late-fifties Custom in 1968, albeit with two pickups only. Then, in 1971, they came up with the so-called 1958 reissue. Still no luck there: they had their own history all wrong and their 1958 was in fact a 1956-style Gold Top with P90s (complete with the tell-tale embossed Gibson logo) and speed knobs. In 1972, the first version of the Custom with the neck "staples" pickup was reissued, followed by the 1955 single-cutaway Special in 1974 (in sunburst – not TV Yellow – with black speed knobs), and the double-cutaway Special in 1976 (this time also available in TV Yellow, but it had a Tune-o-matic instead of the wraparound bridge).

In 1979, the KM (for Kalamazoo) model was as close to a Burst reissue as Gibson had gotten yet. It had exposed cream and zebra T-Top humbuckers and several shades of sunburst. But many details were wrong, from the large headstock with back volute to the three-piece maple neck, and the tops could be two or three-piece and very few of them had any flaming going on.

Suffice to say that historical accuracy was not Gibson's forte yet, and reissuing the Burst did not seem like a priority to them even though many players were asking for it.

So many players were asking for it in fact that a few stores took matters into their own hands. Stores were allowed to order custom guitars directly from Gibson, and all they wanted was a Burst. Some of them got close to that with very exclusive limited runs designed by Strings & Things in Memphis (as early as 1975), then Leo's in Oakland, California, Jimmy Wallace in Dallas, Texas and Guitar Trader in Red Bank, New Jersey.

Finally, in yet another "Okay, you win" situation, Gibson came up with the Heritage series. Two models came out in 1980 with the proper sunbursts (cherry, honey or dark), the right headstock with no volute and the right woods, including some gorgeous two-piece flame tops. Contrary to the "regular" Heritage Standard 80, the Elite had an ebony fretboard. And for those dealers who were selling a lot of instruments from the Heritage series, Gibson had an exclusive third model, the Award, which had gold hardware. The Grover tuners on all three models were an indication of what most players were putting on their regular Bursts at the time, and the whole guitar was believable enough for most players, especially when compared to earlier attempts at reissuing the Burst.

Pickup-wise, Tim Shaw (who had started working for Gibson in 1978) designed a replica of vintage PAFs. Considering the relative lack of available information and materials of the era, those Tim Shaw PAFs from the eighties got pretty close to the goal.

Still, a few specialist stores were asking for something even closer to the real thing, so they would handpick maple tops and create their own custom-made models in very limited quantities. Guitar Trader (New Jersey) did their version in 1982, and the first few orders even came with real PAFs! That would definitely make for a nice Custom Shop reissue concept today.

Those reissues sold for $1,500, while an original at the time could sell for $5,000 up to $7,500 for the nice flamey ones. That huge difference

in price also explains why guitarists and store-owners alike were so eager to get their hands on a proper reissue.

In 1983, the Heritage became the Les Paul Reissue Flametop, and the Gold Top was also reissued that same year (after a short run of 30th Anniversary '57-style Gold Tops). More models were to follow, but the root of the whole reissue trend as we know it today finds its roots right here.

1974 Selmer (Gibson's UK distributor) ad for the Les Paul 1955 Special reissue.

OUT OF SIGHT, OUT OF MIND

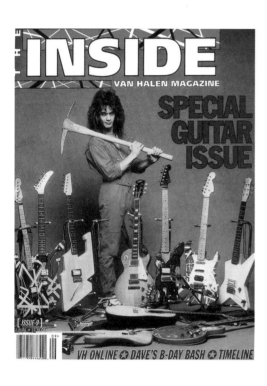

Eddie Van Halen on the cover of *Inside* magazine with his guitar collection in 1979. All his guitars have been heavily modified except for the 1959 Burst that's right in the center.

EVH
FRANKIE STRIPED
MN RELIC
(FRANKENSTRAT
REPLICA)

The undisputed guitar king of the eighties was Eddie Van Halen. When *Van Halen I* came out in 1978, the whole guitar world was turned upside down. No one had ever heard such stunning fretwork, especially on the guitar solo track "Eruption", which in many ways was to the eighties what Led Zeppelin's "Heartbreaker" was to the seventies. From then on, every guitarist had to use tapping in their solos, they needed a modded Marshall amp with extra distortion (even though it turns out Eddie's amps were probably stock at the time), and they needed a visually stunning guitar with a humbucker and a Floyd Rose vibrato (inspired by Eddie and his famous Frankenstrat). Eddie would decorate his guitars himself and heavily modify them to fit his needs, which usually meant leaving only one humbucker in the bridge position. In that respect, he was following in Les Paul's footsteps and, despite their stylistic differences, the two had very similar ways of approaching the guitar merely as a tool that can be changed to perform like it should, a means to a musical end. Van Halen even had an Ibanez Destroyer (a copy of an Explorer) that he literally destroyed, meaning that he actually took a chunk out of it with a bandsaw. But even the ultimate eighties guitarist was not immune to the Burst bug. Since Van Halen used to cover a lot of ZZ Top songs when they started out, it is

TOTO
IV
1982

VAN HALEN
VAN HALEN
1978

very likely that Eddie wanted to capture that Pearly Gates vibe. As soon as he got a record deal, he went to Norman Harris, one of the first and most important vintage guitar dealers in the US: "Eddie used to come into my store before he had a record deal. He used to hang around and kinda look and drool at the guitars. When he first got his deal, he came in and said: "Look, I've wanted a sunburst Les Paul forever." I sold him two of them for $6,500, and this was 1978, maybe 1980. One of them was ultra-flamey."

The flamey one was a '59, and the plain-top one was a '58, but the latter sounded better according to Eddie himself. This is one of the very few guitars that he never really modded. There are a few pictures of him posing with his collection at the time, and one of the Les Paul reigns supreme as the only "clean" guitar in the midst of all the Frankensteins. He only took the neck pickup out of his 1958 when he toured with it, but this is an easily reversible operation, and he would use it live for all the songs that didn't need a vibrato. But even though he was engrossed with those guitars, he remained associated with the Frankenstrat, and the countless players that wanted to imitate him back then would tend to gravitate towards those guitars.

MTV and the radio of the era had an almost compulsory guitar solo in every song, and a lot of those were played by a single person, namely Steve Lukather. Lukather was the guitarist in chart-topping band Toto, but he was also the most in-demand session player of the era, and even though he is now associated with his signature Music Man model (which only came out in the early nineties), he was a Burst player at the time. He had an Ibanez signature model

out in 1981 following a shady endorsement deal (the story goes they built him a prototype but the production model was nothing like it), and sometimes played a Valley Arts superstrat (a California boutique brand born out of a repair shop in 1975), but most of his session work was done on a 1959 Burst, including the legendary "Rosanna" solo on *Toto IV*.

"I used it on so many recordings. I did Lionel Ritchie's "Running with the Night" on that, the riff to [Michael Jackson's] "Beat It,"... a lot of hit records. Basically everything from 1980 to '83 was all the Burst. Well, that and the first Valley Arts guitar."

Just like Jimmy Page's black Custom was everywhere on British radio in the sixties but never seen in the public eye, Lukather's Burst was ubiquitous on the airwaves in the eighties but could not be spotted on MTV.

Steve Lukather with his Ibanez signature model in the 1983 catalog.

Steve Lukather on the cover of the April 1984 issue of *Guitar Player* magazine with his 1959 Burst.

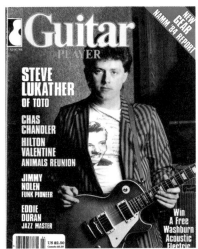

NOT SAFE FOR (M)TV

For all that superstratty nonsense, a few players that became household names in the eighties did choose the Les Paul, but they were usually more leftfield models, or heavily modded ones, and you didn't see them in the videos anyway. Mike Campbell in the early days of Tom Petty and the Heartbreakers had very few guitars: a 1964 sunburst Stratocaster, a 1951 Broadcaster and a 1968 Gold Top reissue with the covers removed from the two P90s, which gave it a very recognizable look. Since Petty would usually borrow the Strat, most of Campbell's parts were recorded with either the Tele or the Gold Top. He still owns it today, but in the meantime, after years of collecting all kinds of guitars, he finally bought a 1959 Burst in the late 2000s. This is the only guitar he used on the 2010 album *Mojo*, and it is responsible for the bluesy sound of the album. Like he says: "It took me 40 years to save up enough money!".

On the other side of the Atlantic, Irish punks U2 were creating their own brand of pop with the help of guitarist The Edge's extensive knowledge of effects. In the videos of the era, he can be seen with a black Strat, but between their second and third albums, he bought a white 1975 Les Paul Custom, which he used as a secret weapon of sorts in the studio:

Neal Schon on the cover of the July 1982 issue of *Guitar Player* magazine, playing his Les Paul Deluxe Pro modded with a Floyd Rose.

"I bought this guitar down on 49th street in New York city in 1982... It was the third guitar I ever bought, after my Explorer and my black Strat. I wanted that Steve Jones *Never Mind The Bollocks...* sound, so I got the same guitar right down to the colour. I never could get that sound, but I found a bunch of songs in this instrument, and have used it extensively ever since, on tour and in the studio." This is the *War* guitar, the one whose fat yet searing sound can be heard on the band's breakthrough single "New Year's Day".

But while Campbell and The Edge kept their Les Pauls stock-ish, some players were trying to make it meet the demands of the era. The Floyd Rose vibrato quickly became the standard when it came out in the late seventies. That system was a double-locking vibrato, meaning the tuners were not in use and the guitar would stay in tune even with extreme use, and also it would fit

The Edge on stage in London with U2 in 2005.

Mike Campbell on
stage with Tom Petty
& The Heartbreakers
in London at the
Hammersmith Odeon
in 1977. He is playing
his 1968 Gold Top.

**TOM PETTY
AND THE
HEARTBREAKERS**
MOJO
2010

inside a recessed cavity in the body of the guitar,
so retrofitting one on a Les Paul would mean
routing a large amount of wood out from the top
and body. Many great Les Pauls have been sacri-
ficed during that period to fit that fashion, but
fortunately Bursts were already getting expensive enough that most players would think twice
about modding them that heavily.

Not all guitars were that lucky though: Neal
Schon, guitarist and mastermind behind the
band Journey, was the second player to get
a production Floyd Rose when they became
available in 1976 (the first one was Eddie Van
Halen, which seems only fair). He took a recent
Les Paul, a black Deluxe Pro, kept the original
cream P90s, and put a Floyd Rose on it. This is
the guitar used on the 1981 classic "Don't Stop
Believing".

While Schon claims to be the first one to
have put a Floyd Rose and a Les Paul together,
Night Ranger's Brad Gillis contests that claim:
he was the third buyer of the new vibrato, and
apparently had it installed on his black Custom
from the early seventies before anyone else did.

All chest-thumping aside, the idea was definitely in the air at the time and many others have
destroyed their beautiful maple tops to accommodate the new must-have vibrato, including
former Gold Top devotee Steve Hackett, who
put a Floyd Rose on a black Les Paul back in
1986. But it was not enough to make the Les Paul
relevant and desirable during that decade. That
was about to change in a major way.

GIBSON
LES PAUL
STANDARD 1981
SUNBURST WITH
KAHLER VIBRATO

This Standard has
been modded with
a Kahler trem, which
at the time was the
alternative to Floyd
Rose.

THAT ONE BURST ON THE MTV

Among the top players of the eighties, Mark Knopfler from Dire Straits is a notable exception for using a sunburst Les Paul on stage during the second half of the decade.

He is associated with the red Stratocaster from the debut single of the band, "Sultans of Swing" in 1978. But by 1985, with Dire Straits now a huge arena-selling act, Knopfler was looking for a new sonic inspiration. He still couldn't yet afford an original Burst, so he bought one of the early eighties reissues and recorded the classic *Brothers in Arms* album with it. This is the guitar we hear on "Money For Nothing" and the one in the half-animation half-live show video that was playing non-stop on MTV at the time. That Les-Paul-through-a-cocked-wah-on-a-Marshall sound was as era-defining as anything.

Knopfler eventually got the Les Paul of his dreams in the nineties. Actually he got two: a very red '59 Burst and a very faded '58. Apparently, the latter is the best-sounding of the two, and this is the one he regularly takes on tour and uses in the studio, so much so that it was replicated by Gibson in 2016 as the Mark Knopfler 1958 Les Paul Standard. This officially made Knopfler one of the very few artists with a Gibson, a Fender and a Martin signature.

Mark Knopfler performing "Money For Nothing" at the Live Aid concert at Wembley Stadium in London, 13th July 1985. He is playing his Burst reissue, and rhythm guitarist Jack Sonni's headless Steinberger guitar can be seen on the left: two very different designs collide.

GIBSON CUSTOM SHOP
MARK KNOPFLER '58 LES PAUL STANDARD

DIRE STRAITS
MONEY FOR NOTHING
1988

PLAY LIST

TOM PETTY AND THE HEARTBREAKERS
Fooled Again (I Don't Like It) (1976)

VAN HALEN
And The Cradle Will Rock (1980)

JOURNEY
Don't Stop Believin' (1981)

TOTO
Rosanna (1982)

MICHAEL JACKSON
Beat It (1982)

U2
New Year's Day (1983)

DIRE STRAITS
Money for Nothing (1985)

50 SHADES OF BURST

Here are a few shades of sunburst as identified by the Gibson Custom Shop. These have been precisely defined in order for customers to request the exact shade they like. Back in the 1950s, most original Bursts came in a vibrant Cherry Sunburst, but some of them differed slightly and they have all aged differently depending on their exposure to sunlight. Collectors have made up some names to define them, and these were adopted by Gibson later on.

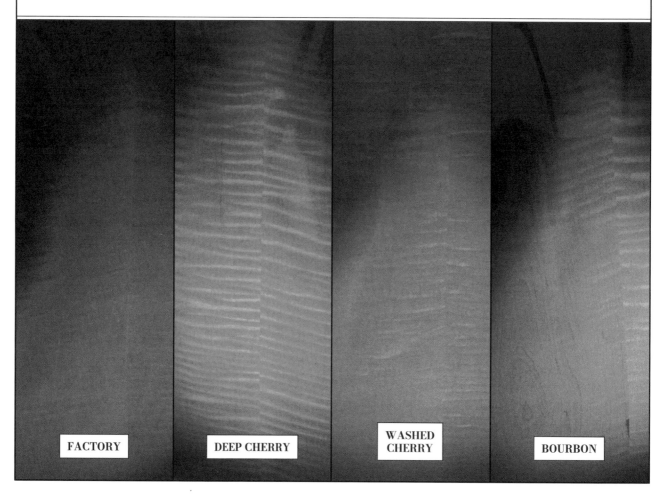

FACTORY

DEEP CHERRY

WASHED CHERRY

BOURBON

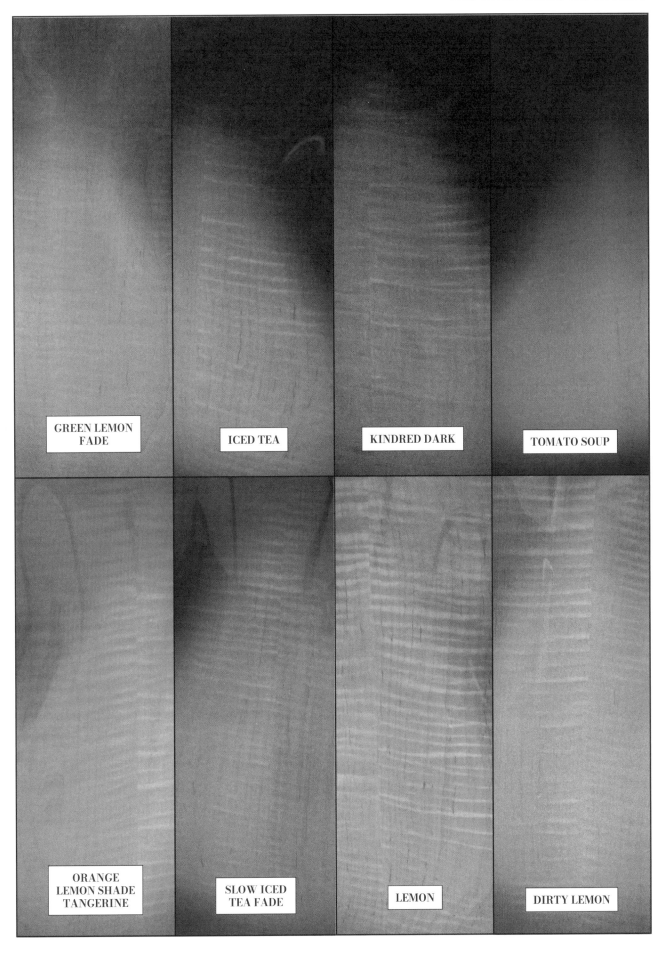

I WAS PROBABLY DRAWN TO THE SHAPE OF IT FIRST, AND THEN I STARTED NOTICING THAT CERTAIN GUITAR PLAYERS WHOSE MUSIC I REALLY LIKED PLAYED THAT GUITAR.

Slash

BACK WITH A VENGEANCE

Once again, Gibson found itself in a very delicate situation in the mid-eighties. The company could have disappeared at that time, and, in spite of some efforts to keep up with the trends of the day with pointy guitars like the XPL, Gibson guitars were not in fashion. The Les Paul seemed like a relic of a time gone by, and many players were trading them for Jacksons and Charvels. It all changed overnight with the band that defined the end of the era: Guns N' Roses.

IT'S COMPLICATED

Gibson opened their Nashville factory in 1974, and over the next decade it became the main production facility while the historic Kalamazoo location was only used for Custom Shop-style orders, archtops, banjos and mandolins. By the early eighties, the Kalamazoo factory only had 44 workers left (there had been as many as 1,600 employees working there in the sixties),

GIBSON
LES PAUL JIMMY
PAGE 1996

and the facility was not in a good state having not really been upgraded or cared for since the Norlin takeover. Paying for two plants at the same time was not a smart business decision, and in 1983 Gibson decided to close the Kalamazoo factory. Jim Deurloo, who was managing the location, wanted to prove that keeping Kalamazoo open was a viable option, but the writing was on the wall. The factory started building Gibsons in 1917, and built the first Les Pauls, Bursts and many other golden-era guitars, but it finally closed on 29th June 1984. Most of the workers had built their homes and families in Michigan, so were not prepared to make the move to Tennessee. As a result, some of them decided to start their own guitar company in the old factory, and to this day the Heritage Guitar Company still builds instruments out of 225 Parsons Street.

In the meantime, Norlin had been trying to get rid of Gibson, which by 1980 had turned into a dead weight in their printing-oriented portfolio. They finally reached an agreement with a trio of buyers in 1986. Henry Juszkiewicz, David Berryman and Gary Zebrowski had already teamed up to acquire the electronics company Phi Technology in Oklahoma City, and they had turned that failing business into a prosperous one. The three of them were Harvard Business School classmates, and Juszkiewicz was the guitarist of the bunch, which got him interested in turning things around for Gibson. Henry became the president, David the vice-president, and Gary stayed focused on Phi Technology. They bought Gibson for just five million dollars, which gives some idea of how badly the company was doing at the time.

Very quickly, Juszkiewicz showed what he was made of with a very aggressive management style. He started out by firing many key people, including the Nashville plant manager and the quality control manager. The goal was to turn a failing company into a profitable one, just like he had done with Phi, and the way to do that was by building the best guitars they could make. Gibsons of the late seventies and early eighties are not the pinnacle of the brand: the available woods were heavy and not too resonant, and the build quality was lacking. Of course, this was mostly down to management choices and not a personal decision by the plant manager. As employee Mark Salhgren recalls: "To me and the people that I worked with, we cared more about the instruments than the corporate, the top people. We cared about every instrument as a creative piece of art. But someone would come through and say you have to finish 100 guitars in a day and you could just see the conflict."

No matter whose fault the failing quality of guitars was, heads had to roll, and Juszkiewicz wanted to make a point. From then on, most employees had to report to Henry about their daily tasks, with the new boss closely controlling the new guitars that were coming out of the factory.

In the same dual movement that had spawned both the Les Paul Junior and the Custom in 1954, Gibson decided to develop its line both in the budget section and in the upper tier. For the cost-conscious players, Japanese brands had already started flooding the market in the early seventies. These brands were copying vintage Les Pauls before Gibson had even started reissuing them, and they were much cheaper than their US-made counterparts. The situation was so problematic that in 1977, Norlin filed a lawsuit against Japanese brand Ibanez to stop them from using the Gibson headstock shape. The lawsuit was settled out of court, but it did not stop many builders from offering very close copies of the classic guitars. Since Gibson could not beat them, they joined them: they started using the Epiphone brand for their Eastern production, keeping the Gibson-branded guitars fully American-made. Juszkiewicz tasked R&D genius Tim Shaw with overseeing Korean production, which in retrospect was probably a smart move since those Epiphones have always been seen as great guitars for a very good price. In 1988, Gibson also launched the Orville brand, named after Gibson

founder Orville Gibson. These were a line of very well-crafted copies from Japan that were reserved for the Japanese market, even though a few of them made it out of the country.

On the other side of the pricing spectrum, Juszkiewicz hired California luthier J.T. Riboloff in 1987 to run the Custom Shop. From then on, the Custom Shop was a separate division within the company, and that division had three main tasks: to act as an R&D department by working on new designs, to build the best possible vintage reissues, and to develop instruments in partnership with endorsed artists. This started with the Jimmy Page model in 1995, then the Joe Perry Boneyard Les Paul in 1996, the Ace Frehley Les Paul and the Slash Les Paul in 1997. While Page, Perry and Frehley were heritage artists who had lived their glory days in the seventies, Slash was a relative newcomer, but in a way he was even more deserving of a signature model than the other three.

Henry Juszkiewicz and Slash in 2007. Note the HD 6X Pro banner behind them, a nice symbol of the divide between the former's vision and the latter's rock n' roll ethos.

1998 Gibson ad for the Joe Perry signature model.

SLASH

KING OF THE IMPOSSIBLE

Slash was the biggest thing to happen to rock guitar since Jimmy Page. In fact, Guns N' Roses took a big page out of the Led Zeppelin and Aerosmith playbooks, with their iconic duo of a high-octane lead singer strutting around the stage and a dark mysterious lead guitarist hidden behind a long wall of hair. But the L.A. band GNR, as they would become known, made the whole thing more edgy, more dangerous, and reminded the world that rock n' roll could be a drug-and-sex-fueled experience. And of course, most of it revolved around the guitar: Slash and rhythm guitarist Izzy Stradlin had developed a simpatico twin-guitar assault worthy of the best Keith Richards/Mick Taylor or Joe Perry/Brad Whitford tracks. And the cherry on top was Slash's lead playing, a fluid fiery melodic style that could hold its own against the shredders of the era but still displayed a strong blues influence and a warm sticky tone that could only come from a Les Paul. The first Guns N' Roses single (with MTV video) from the debut *Appetite For Destruction* album was "Welcome To The Jungle", and in the video Slash, already a fully-formed guitar hero with his top hat, was playing a sunburst Les Paul, which was a complete anomaly in those days. Tom Keifer, singer and guitarist of the Philadelphia band Cinderella, was the only one who played his '59 Burst in a current band at the time, but Slash came along and instantly made the Les Paul cool again, maybe even cooler than it had ever been. Henry Juszkiewicz had only been in office for a year and a half but his brand was definitely back, in a way even he could not have foreseen, especially with the band's 1987 number-one single, "Sweet Child O'Mine". The video was being played several times a day on MTV, and Slash would be playing a Les Paul every time!

Slash with his favorite 1987 Les Paul Standard "Jessica". He is playing at the Wembley Stadium for the Freddie Mercury Tribute Concert on 20th April 1992. Brian May's Red Special appears behind him.

GIBSON
SLASH LES
PAUL STANDARD
ANACONDA BURST

Nineties Gibson ad featuring Slash with his 1987 Standard.

Only a Gibson is Good Enough.

Slash saved the Les Paul, but he did it with two copies. His very first guitar was a Memphis brand Les Paul copy (made in Japan), the very guitars that Gibson was trying to fight off with their Epiphone brand, and the guitar he used on the first album was a Burst replica built by a luthier. Still, this is the one that gave Les Paul envy to a whole generation.

The beginning of Slash's infatuation with the Les Paul was a visual thing, but sound quickly caught up:

"The Les Paul was always cool-looking for me. When I was a little kid, way before I had any aspiration of being a guitar player we had the *Led Zeppelin II* record. I've always loved music, I just didn't have any designs on being a musician. So I listened to a lot of stuff and that particular record I loved the sound of it. So when I did pick up a guitar and equated that that was a Les Paul, that was a huge bonus. I was like, 'Oh, okay; so this is the right guitar then.'"

When GNR entered the studio to record what would become *Appetite For Destruction*, Slash did not have his good guitars anymore. He used to have a Burst replica built by Max Baranet that had belonged to Alice Cooper and Lou Reed guitarist Steve Hunter beforehand, and he had a Jackson, but legend has it that he sold those two in order to fund a drug habit. He only had a B.C. Rich Warlock that didn't really cut the mustard, so manager Alan Niven went to a store and bought a '59 replica made by luthier Kris Derrig. Since the guitar didn't have any pickup installed at that point, Niven bought two zebra Seymour

SLASH'S SNAKEPIT
IT'S FIVE O'CLOCK SOMEWHERE
1995

GUNS N' ROSES
APPETITE FOR DESTRUCTION
1987

185

LES PAUL

GIBSON
BUCKETHEAD SIGNATURE LES PAUL

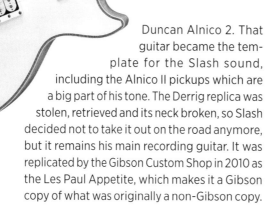

The red switch tip and arcade-style kill switch make the Buckethead Les Paul instantly recognizable.

GIBSON CUSTOM SHOP
SLASH "FIRST STANDARD" 58 LES PAUL

Duncan Alnico 2. That guitar became the template for the Slash sound, including the Alnico II pickups which are a big part of his tone. The Derrig replica was stolen, retrieved and its neck broken, so Slash decided not to take it out on the road anymore, but it remains his main recording guitar. It was replicated by the Gibson Custom Shop in 2010 as the Les Paul Appetite, which makes it a Gibson copy of what was originally a non-Gibson copy.

On the amp front, Slash was following in the glorious footsteps of Clapton, Page and Perry by using Marshall stacks. *Appetite For Destruction* was recorded with a modded plexi, but soon he switched to a Silver Jubilee, a limited-edition released in 1987 with a lot more gain than your usual plexi. This remains the magical Slash combination, and it took the "Les Paul and Marshall" combo into more modern territory, with enough gain to play metal-influenced palm muted riffs and speedy licks.

After the release of the album, Slash picked two nearly-identical brand-new 1987 Les Paul Standards directly from Gibson, and modded them to his typical specs, i.e. Seymour Duncan Alnico 2 pickups and no pickguard. These two were his main guitars throughout the band's first world tour from August 1987 to December 1988.

Slash's first signature model in 1996 was based on the cover art of his first album with his solo band Slash's Snakepit, the hard-blues classic *It's Five O'Clock Somewhere*. It is a red flame-top Les Paul with the album cover top-hat snake on the body and a snake inlay in the fretboard. Only a hundred of these were made and they remain very collectible today. That same year, Slash was also the recipient of Marshall's first

signature amp ever, the 2555SL JCM Slash which was based on the Silver Jubilee.

It makes sense that every brand under the sun would want to make a signature model with Slash, since he was absolutely everywhere at the time, on the cover of every possible music magazine and on posters in every teenager's bedroom. He was in many ways the last guitar hero of that magnitude. Millions started playing the guitar out of admiration and fascination for the top-hatted hero, and GNR was the biggest band on earth. However, 1996 was already the beginning of the end for the band as people knew it, and because of growing tensions between Slash and singer Axl Rose, the former quit the band. While Slash was playing in Velvet Revolver and his solo projects, Axl Rose kept the band going with other guitarists, and most of them were also playing Les Pauls, since that was the definitive GNR sound and look.

Buckethead joined the band in 2000, and even though he had previously been using pointy Jacksons and ESPs, he instantly became a Les Paul player, with a full-white Custom-made model featuring white hardware and pickup rings, and a slightly bigger body to match his massive stature (6'5"). This white whale finally became a signature model in 2009, with an extended scale length of 27" (instead of the usual 24.75"), 24 frets, and a chambered over-sized body. It is all white, with only two red kill switches that look like videogame arcade buttons. This highly distinctive model became significantly cheaper when it was turned into the Les Paul Studio Buckethead, with nearly-identical features and a satin finish.

Bumblefoot (a member of GNR from 2006 to 2014) had been a faithful Vigier player since

Slash eventually returned to the fold in 2016 for the aptly named "Not In This Lifetime... Tour", and with that reunion of sorts GNR has regained its status as one of the biggest rock bands in the world.

To this day, Slash has collaborated with Gibson on no fewer than sixteen signature models, most of them variations on the "Les Paul with two Alnico 2 pickups" theme, but also some unexpected ideas, such as a Firebird model (albeit with a maple top and the same pickups, 2017), a black double-neck SG (2019) and a J-45 acoustic (2020). Among all these models, one of them is extra special: a 2017 Custom Shop replica of one of Slash's 1958 Bursts called the Les Paul First Standard. Slash had already been the owner of this '58 (serial number 8 3096) for a while when he found out that it was actually the first Cherry Sunburst Les Paul with a two-piece-center-seamed top, a guitar that was used at the NAMM Show in July 1958 to showcase the new color to dealers! Hence the name "First Standard". This would have been a hugely significant guitar under any circumstance, but the fact that it also happens to belong to the man who brought the Les Paul back, almost from the dead, is a very moving full-circle story.

In 2020, Gibson and Slash took their relationship even further by launching the Slash Collection, a full line of Slash guitars including several regular USA-made models alongside the usual Custom Shop limited editions. Slash even has Epiphone models to his name. He is the first artist with his own collection of models, which shows just how important he is to the brand.

GIBSON CUSTOM SHOP

SLASH SIGNATURE "SNAKEPIT" LES PAUL 1996

1998, but he still used a Les Paul when he was in the band: "My first electric was an imitation sunburst Les Paul in '78 at the age of 8. I finally got a real Les Paul in '89, a re-issue of the '59 with Les Paul's signature on the pickguard. With any song, any band, you want the guitar that fits. With GNR I included the Les Paul in my arsenal, it was the appropriate sound and style for their classic songs."

The first Slash signature model ever, leaning against Slash's first signature amp, the JCM Slash.

2022 Gibson ad for the new "Number 4" Slash Les Paul.

GIBSON CUSTOM SHOP

SLASH SIGNATURE "APPETITE FOR DESTRUCTION" LES PAUL

BIRTHDAY BURST

In 1980, guitarist Joe Perry had left Aerosmith, and money was becoming an issue. He needed to sell gear, and his 1959 dark Burst was an obvious choice since it would sell quickly and for a good price. Texas guitarist Eric Johnson ended up buying the instrument, and he made Perry an offer if he wanted to buy it back, but the Aerosmith man could not afford it at the time.

Meanwhile, Slash was making waves with Guns N' Roses, and he had been deeply touched by this very same guitar, having seen it pictured inside the gatefold of the 1978 Aerosmith live album *Official Bootleg*. Slash has turned the darker shade of sunburst "tobacco burst" into a signature color of sorts through several of his own models, and most of that infatuation can be traced back to the Joe Perry Burst: "That was the coolest guitar I'd ever seen. Years and years later, I was in Japan I got this phone call, saying that there's some guy trying to sell this guitar that I might be interested in, and it was a '59 Tobacco Les Paul, owned by Duane Allman and Joe Perry... So I said, 'Send me the photos!' We were on tour in Japan so when I got back to L.A. I went to my apartment and there was this envelope, I just opened it up sort of nonchalantly, and out came these 3x5s of this guitar... I recognized the guitar from hours of studying the pictures [in the gatefold vinyl of Aerosmith's *Live Bootleg*]. I bought the guitar for eight grand, nobody knew exactly what the value of these were."

By the time Aerosmith had made their comeback, Perry could afford to buy the guitar back but he didn't know who the owner was. His Aerosmith guitarist partner Brad Whitford found the mystery guitar in a magazine photo of Slash and the Burst, but Slash didn't want to let that guitar go. It was too important and historically significant for him to part with.

"It was sort of a coveted thing for me, I really didn't touch it too much. A few years later, I went into the studio, I was making a record and I pulled this thing out. Which is what happens with vintage guitars, you tend to tuck them away... I pulled this thing out, and it sounded really good, but it didn't sound like anything to write home about. So I recorded one song with it, shot one video with it ("November Rain" by Guns N' Roses in 1991), and then years and years went by and finally I gave it back to Joe for his birthday. "

In 2000, Perry turned fifty, and he was playing with the band Cheap Trick for his birthday party when his guitar tech approached him with an old familiar friend: Slash had finally decided to give it back to him as a birthday gift.

That triple signature guitar (Les Paul, Joe Perry, Slash) was finally replicated by the Custom Shop in 2013.

As Slash puts it: "It's a good guitar, but it didn't speak to me in the way that my own guitar did." His choice of words is extremely interesting here. Slash's Burst wasn't "his own guitar". Even though he had been its owner for a number of years, it remained Joe Perry's guitar and had to return to its rightful owner after all.

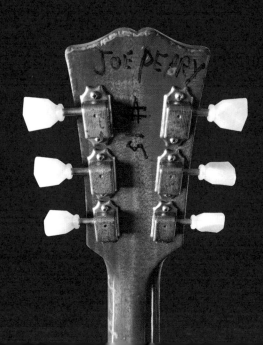

Gibson Custom Shop Joe Perry / Slash '59 Les Paul Aged and Signed.

The wear under the neck pickup volume makes that guitar even more special.

METAL HEALTH

OZZY OSBOURNE
BLIZZARD OF OZZ
1980

Iron Maiden during the 1985 Australian leg of the gigantic World Slavery Tour (189 shows in 11 months!). Bassist Steve Harris and guitarist Adrian Smith with his Gold Top Deluxe.

Thanks to Slash, lots of players discovered how perfect the Les Paul was for a heavily distorted sound. The guitar was an amazing rock axe, but it also happened to perfectly fit the bill for another style that had not been invented way back in 1952: heavy metal. It wasn't always an obvious choice, but many classic metal albums have been recorded with a Les Paul.

It all started in 1974, when Irish rock band Thin Lizzy released their fourth album, *Nightlife*. Before that, the band was a power trio that revolved around bassist Phil Lynott's beautiful voice, but from 1974 on, Thin Lizzy became the vessel for the dual-guitar harmonies of Brian Robertson and Scott Gorham, culminating in 1976 with the album *Jailbreak* and the timeless classic "The Boys Are Back In Town". The two of them had nearly-identical Les Paul Deluxes from the seventies, a redder one with no pickguard for Gorham and a slightly darker one for Robertson.

British metalheads Iron Maiden were among the bands that were deeply influenced by the

guitar harmonies of Thin Lizzy, and Adrian Smith, their second guitarist who joined the band for its second album in 1980, was also using a Deluxe. His was a 1972 Gold Top Deluxe that he bought in 1974, his first "proper" guitar that he still owns, uses and loves to this day. He replaced the bridge pickup with a DiMarzio Super Distortion, but the neck pickup remains a mini humbucker.

In 1980, singer Ozzy Osbourne released his first album after having been fired from Black Sabbath, *Blizzard of Ozz*. On the guitar front, he had enlisted the services of a strapping young Californian gunslinger fresh out of his previous band, Quiet Riot. Randy Rhoads had a unique sound and a unique style, unlike any other metal guitarist of the era. He was as fast and virtuosic as Eddie Van Halen, but his riffs and sound were heavier and his solos had a classical flavor to them, courtesy of Rhoads being classically trained and extremely proficient on the nylon-string guitar. In 1972, Randy Rhoads saw David Bowie in concert in his hometown of Santa Monica, and was completely stunned by the animal grace of guitarist Mick Ronson. Rhoads adopted a hairstyle very close to Ronson's, and two years later bought the same guitar, a 1974 cream Les Paul Custom. It quickly became his favorite guitar, and he kept on playing it alongside Ozzy even after designing his Charvel/ Jackson model, the pointy Flying V that still bears his name to this day. Rhoads tragically died in a plane crash while on tour at the age of 25, just a few months after the release of his second album with Ozzy, *Diary of a Madman* (1981).

After a couple of albums featuring the Charvel-fueled pyrotechnics of Jake E. Lee, Ozzy found a replacement with the 21 year-old New-Jersey born Zakk Wylde, another player with a highly personal approach and an instantly recognizable left-hand vibrato. When he joined

Randy Rhoads on stage in 1981 with his Custom and a python skin strap.

Zakk Wylde on stage with The Grail, his main Custom.

Ozzy's band in 1987, he bought a cream 1981 Les Paul Custom with a maple neck but since that guitar was visually too close to Rhoads', he asked a luthier to paint the spiral from the poster for the Hitchcock movie *Vertigo*, which did not go according to plan, so when Wylde picked up the guitar it had target-style black and white concentric circles on the Les Paul's top. Even though it originally was an accident, it became Zakk's signature "bullseye" motif, which was replicated on his signature models. That 1981 Custom was nicknamed "The Grail", and it received a pair of active EMG pickups (bridge 81 and neck 85) which were perfect for Wylde's pinched harmonics.

Wylde has enjoyed an on again/off again relationship with Ozzy Osbourne while fronting his own band, Black Label Society, with great success. In 1999, he received his first signature model, the Zakk Wylde Bullseye, followed by the camouflage version, the Camo Bullseye, in 2004. He also designed a few Epiphone signature models, and just like Slash he also got his Marshall signature, the 2203ZW, making them the only two artists to have both a Les Paul and a Marshall to their name.

Poster for the movie *Vertigo*.

OZZY OSBOURNE

DIARY OF A MADMAN

1981

THIN LIZZY
JAILBREAK
1976

GIBSON
ZAKK WYLDE LES PAUL CUSTOM BULLSEYE

EPIPHONE
LES PAUL CUSTOM ZAKK WYLDE BULLSEYE CAMO

STILL CRAZY AFTER ALL THESE YEARS

GIBSON
CUSTOM SHOP
JERRY CANTRELL
"WINO" LES PAUL
CUSTOM

JERRY CANTRELL
DEGRADATION
TRIP
2002

Back in 1983, a few years before the company changed hands, Gibson created a very important model that is still part of today's catalog: the Les Paul Studio. The Studio was a brilliantly simple design, meant to keep what was important about the Standard and dispose of any superfluous element, which is why it had no binding whatsoever, and why it had dot inlays and a Junior-style decal headstock logo. The carved maple top on a mahogany body was still there, and so were the two humbuckers. The Studio was a success and it has been through many variations and revisions, such as the Studio Standard (1984, with bound body and fretboard), the Studio Custom (1984, with gold hardware), the revised Studio (1990, with crown inlays), the Studio Gem (1996, with P90 pickups and gold hardware), the Studio Gothic (2001, all black including hardware, with an ebony fretboard), the Studio Plus (2001, with figured top and gold hardware), the Studio Premier Plus (2006, with extra figured top and gold hardware), the Studio Baritone (2004, with a longer scale to be tuned down) and the Studio Raw Power (2009, with maple fretboard). And just like the Custom Lite that came out in 1987, there also was a Studio Lite in 1988 to solve the age-old issue of the weight of the Les Paul over a guitar player's shoulder. They had thinner bodies with contouring, and the second version of the Studio Lite in 1990 even had an insert of balsa wood into the mahogany to relieve the weight. This is also the time when Gibson started chambering their bodies or designing thinner models to gain a few grams, which led to a hot debate between players as to whether or not it made a palpable difference in sound.

The Les Paul Classic 1960, launched in 1990, was one of the most interesting new additions to the Gibson lineup. It was designed by J.T. Riboloff of the Custom Shop in an attempt to make a reissue that would not cost an arm and a leg. It was built by the regular USA factory, but it featured most of the specs that made the Burst special, including the smaller headstock, Kluson-style tuners, bell knobs, cream plastic parts and a slim-taper early-sixties-style neck. The only unexpected feature was a set of uncovered ceramic pickups (496R and 500T) that had a much hotter output level than your regular PAF. Either the player would replace them with one of the many PAF replicas available out there, or they would fully embrace that ceramic tone for heavy riffs and scorching leads that Clapton could have only dreamt of back in 1965.

Guns N' Roses was right in the middle ground between eighties kitsch and nineties cool, but after them a whole new generation of rock

Jerry Cantrell on stage with Alice In Chains in 2016. He is playing "Wino", his Wine Red Les Paul Custom.

GIBSON
CUSTOM SHOP
ADAM JONES
1979 LES PAUL
CUSTOM ANTIQUE
SILVERBURST

GIBSON
LES PAUL STUDIO
2022 TANGERINE
BURST

More and more players had been requesting the Silverburst finish on Custom Shop guitars prior to the release of the Adam Jones model.

players embraced the new-found coolness of the Les Paul. The grunge wave from Seattle was all about cheaper guitars, such as Nirvana's Kurt Cobain's Fender Mustang or Soundgarden's Kim Thayil's Guild S-100, a weird offset copy of the SG. But even though it was on the more expensive side, the massive sound of the Les Paul made it a no-brainer for grunge artists looking to make their riffs as heavy as possible.

Buzz Osborne from sludge trio The Melvins was a major influence for that scene, and he played a mid-seventies Black Beauty plugged into a transistor amp for maximum damage. Jerry Cantrell from Alice In Chains followed in King Buzzo's illustrious footsteps by choosing Les Paul Customs for the second part of his career. His most notable guitar was a white Les Paul Custom with cigarette-burn-spots all over the body, an instrument that was exclusively and extensively used to write the songs for Cantrell's second solo album, *Degradation Trip* (2002). Fittingly for such an incredibly dark album, the Les Paul had its headstock broken during the process, but apparently it was still playable, so Cantrell still used it in that sorry state and didn't bother fixing it until much later. In 2021, Cantrell finally got a Gibson signature model, a Custom Shop replica of his favorite wine-red Custom, the "Wino".

Left page
Adam Jones playing with Tool in 1997. He is playing his trusty 1979 Les Paul Custom Silverburst.

**GIBSON
CUSTOM SHOP**
LES PAUL CUSTOM
SILVERBURST 2017

LES PAUL

GIBSON
LES PAUL
CLASSIC 2007

Chris Cornell from Soundgarden was also a Custom devotee, and could be seen with a highly unusual finish debuted by Gibson in 1987, the silverburst. That strange color fading from black to a greenish shade of silver was only available on the Les Paul Custom, and it caught the imagination of a few players. Adam Jones from the progressive metal band Tool turned it into his 2021 signature model (complete with silverburst case!), modeled after his favorite 1979 silverburst Custom nicknamed "The Witness". In 2022, he turned his Custom Shop model into a regular USA model by introducing the Adam Jones Les Paul Standard Antique Silverburst, which represents the first time that finish has been used on a Standard. More recently, Bill Kelliher from the progressive sludge band Mastodon has also been relying on his Les Paul Custom Silverburst, which gave the idea to his bandmate Brent Hinds who designed a Custom-style silverburst Flying V as his signature model.

Finally, grunge heroes Pearl Jam also played on a bunch of Les Pauls, mostly Black Beauties and Gold Tops. Stone Gossard has played his share of cool Les Pauls, but his partner Mike McCready took the cake with a Grover-equipped '59 Burst he bought in 1998. That Burst had belonged to Jim Armstrong, who was playing in the Irish rock band Them in the sixties, alongside singer Van Morrison, and it has been replicated by the Custom Shop in 2016 as the Mike McCready 1959 Les Paul Standard.

McCready paid $25,000 for his Standard, and back in 1998 the Burst fever was only getting started. The Grunge hero was part of one of the biggest bands of the era, yet he somehow was ahead of the pack by rediscovering what incredible instruments those Les Pauls were.

The "1960" on the pickguard alludes to the neck on this model: it is as slim as a 1960 Burst.

GIBSON CUSTOM SHOP

MIKE MCCREADY '59 LES PAUL STANDARD

PLAY LIST

THIN LIZZY
Jailbreak (1976)

OZZY OSBOURNE
Mr Crowley (1980)

GUNS N' ROSES
Welcome To The Jungle (1987)

OZZY OSBOURNE
Miracle Man (1988)

THE MELVINS
Hooch (1993)

SLASH'S SNAKEPIT
Beggars and Hangers-On (1995)

TOOL
Hooker with a Penis (1996)

PEARL JAM
Breakerfall (2000)

IRON MAIDEN
Wicker Man (2000)

MASTODON
The Wolf is Loose (2006)

ALICE IN CHAINS
Check My Brain (2009)

IT'S A PHENOMENON
TO HAVE SOMETHING LAST
THIS LONG, AND THERE ARE A LOT
OF FINE POINTS THAT SPEAK
TO THE LES PAUL'S LONGEVITY.
BUT THE MOST IMPORTANT
FACTOR IS ITS BEAUTY – IT HAS
A BEAUTIFUL LOOK AND
A BEAUTIFUL SOUND. A LES PAUL
IS YOUR BEST FRIEND,
YOUR SPOUSE, YOUR PARTNER,
IT'S EVERYTHING TO YOU.
YOU CAN'T FIND A MORE
GORGEOUS INSTRUMENT.
THE OTHERS ARE JUST PLANKS
OF WOOD.

Les Paul

A NEW GOLDEN AGE?

History has a way of repeating itself, and for the Les Paul the noughties were not unlike the eighties: rock music was not as present in mainstream media, and the bands that were part of the zeitgeist were either indie garage artists playing Fenders or pawn-shop brands like Silvertone and Kay, or nü-metal darlings with seven-string Ibanez models. Gibson did make a seven-string Les Paul, but it wasn't enough to make the brand part of the conversation. And some less-than-ideal business decisions did not help the brand's case at the time either.

But a few unwavering faithfuls were still turning heads with the age-old single-cutaway guitar design, and nowadays, in the early 2020s, it seems like a new era is starting for Gibson, a new golden age for a design that has managed to remain highly desirable through the decades.

OLD FLAMES

A few best-selling artists and fan favorites have made the choice of playing Les Pauls in the 2000s, at a time when the model was not exactly on everyone's mind.

GIBSON
PAUL LANDERS
SIGNATURE
LES PAUL

Back in 2003, Metallica was not in the best possible shape either: the stadium-filling metal band was coming apart at the seams and, as can be seen in the documentary *Some Kind Of Monster*, they came dangerously close to breaking up at that point. Still, they managed to produce one of their most controversial albums, *Saint Anger*, a rough-sounding hard-riffing affair with nary a solo to be heard. Even though soloist Kirk Hammett had occasionally been playing a black Custom since the late-eighties, it's riffmeister James Hetfield who introduced an extremely cool hot-rodded version of the Custom for the tour and "Frantic" video that followed the release of the album. His 1973 Black Beauty was modded with two EMG pickups (81 in the bridge position, 85 in the neck position, the classic Metallica/Zakk Wylde setup), a huge Iron Cross behind the bridge, a large chunk of paint missing on the lower bout of the body, and a gold racing stripe above the pickups. A looker for sure. Ironically, ESP, which has endorsed Hetfield since the late-eighties, has

This rare model was only made in 2012 and it is probably the simplest a Les Paul Standard can get with just one volume knob and no poker chip.

NEVER DIE

James Hetfield pummeling his Iron Cross Les Paul with Metallica in 2003.

released an Iron Cross signature model in 2008 that looks extremely similar to the 1973 Custom. Hetfield has never played them on stage, but he also owns four Bursts as part of his collection (one '58, two '59s and a '60).

Kirk Hammett finally managed to outdo Hetfield's Les Paul swag in 2014, when he bought Greeny, the '59 Burst formerly owned by Peter Green and Gary Moore (*see* page 157). He used it extensively on the 2016 Metallica album *Hardwired... To Self-Destruct*, but most importantly he has also been playing it a lot on stages around the world for more than 200 shows to this day. That particular guitar has some serious mileage, and the Kalamazoo craftsman who made it back in 1959 couldn't have dreamt of such a glorious fate for his creation.

By the time Hetfield modded his Custom in 2003, Zakk Wylde had already turned the Custom-with-EMG-pickups into a tried-and-true metal stalwart.

Paul Landers from German indus metal kings Rammstein picked a very stark and cold satin-finished black Les Paul with chrome parts and no poker chips for his 2012 signature model, with EMGs of course.

Guitarist Björn Gelotte from Swedish melodic death metal pioneers In Flames fell in love with a black Custom modded with EMGs in the early 2000s. The music by that Göteborg band

ESP
JAMES HETFIELD IRON CROSS

Poster for the movie *Some Kind of Monster.*

METALLICA
ST. ANGER
2003

became so influential to so many other bands that Gelotte finally got a signature Epiphone model in 2005, a gorgeous Black Beauty featuring the same set of pickups as his original with the split diamond on the headstock shaped like In Flames' Jester symbol.

The choice of doing an Epiphone signature instead of a much more expensive Gibson version comes down to the typical audience of metal bands at the time, which were mostly younger adults with limited budgets. Other brands had already developed those cheaper metal signature models, especially ESP with the LTD brand and countless best-selling Metallica models.

The reasoning was the same for Trivium's Matt Heafy's signature Epiphone Custom in 2013, a black Custom with EMG pickups available in 6- or 7-string versions. But metal fans have grown up, and some of them have become affluent collectors and are still fans of their favorite bands, a perfect example of that being the sold-out $10 000 Adam Jones Les Paul Custom silverburst replica released in 2021.

EPIPHONE
BJÖRN GELOTTE
LES PAUL CUSTOM

EPIPHONE
MATT HEAFY LES PAUL
CUSTOM ORIGINS

Björn Gelotte on stage
with In Flames in 2008.

KIRK HAMMETT ON GREENY

In 2014, Kirk Hammett of Metallica bought one of the most important Les Pauls that ever was: the Peter Green/Gary Moore '59 Burst. It was the first of the Collector's Choice Series and will soon most likely be replicated a second time by the Custom Shop, since their cloning technology has really come into its own during the past decade.

In 2020, Dean DelRay of the podcast *Let There Be Talk* sat with Hammett to discuss his historic guitar:

"It's really crazy because it feels like this guitar came to me. I had been in London for a couple of days when I got a call from a friend of mine who's a guitar dealer. He said, 'I have a guitar for you to check out.' I said, 'Okay, what's the guitar?' He said, 'Greeny'. I said, 'Bro, I'm not interested in a guitar with a price tag of two million dollars.' And he said, 'Nah it's all poppycock, it's not two million dollars, it's not even one million dollars, it's all rumor.' And I was like, 'Mmm, okay, maybe you should bring it over'. And he brought it to my hotel room, with an amazing amp, which didn't help... That old Vox that sounded incredible, with these ghost notes, like you're hearing other notes other than what you're playing, it happens with old vintage stuff. I had that guitar in my hand for maybe a minute and a half, and I just knew bro, I just freakin' knew. I wasn't gonna give it back. I was not going to give it back.

"And what blew me away was: I plugged it in and I hit a chord on the bridge pickup, nice and clear, it cuts, and then I switched to the neck pickup and start playing some lead stuff and I went, 'Oh my god, man, super syrupy, creamy tone', and then I put it in the middle – and this is what makes this guitar so unusual, the fact that the neck pickup is turned around so the screws are facing towards the middle rather than towards the neck – because it's like that, it creates an out of phase sound that sounds like a Strat through a 100w Marshall, and I could not believe that sound. I thought, 'That's not supposed to happen man, a Les Paul turning into a Strat at the flick of a switch'. It was amazing. It hadn't even come into consideration, who owned it and who had played it, I was just blown away by the fact that it was just a super, super musical, incredibly tonally gifted piece of wood. There's a term for that, a four letter word, and it's called mojo. The mojo connected to this piece of wood is just out of control."

Kirk Hammett on stage with Greeny in 2017 during a Metallica concert in their hometown of San Francisco.

BRAND NEW LES PAULS

Gibson
Custom Shop Les Paul Special Double-Cut Figured Top

This is an attempt at describing the Les Paul line as of 2022. There are three main levels: Epiphone, Gibson USA and Gibson Custom Shop, and with every level comes a variety of Les Pauls with specs that go from forward-thinking models to vintage-correct reissues.

EPIPHONE

Les Paul Standard '50s: post-'57 Standard specs

Les Paul Standard '60s: same with a slim taper neck

Les Paul Custom: all-mahogany body Custom with two humbuckers and slim neck

Les Paul Classic Worn: "worn finish" and uncovered zebra pickups

Les Paul Junior: single-cut version of the Junior

Les Paul Special: single-cut version of the Special

Les Paul Studio: basically a Standard with no bindings

Les Paul Express: a mini Les Paul

Les Paul Melody Maker E1: minimal decoration, bolt-on neck, all-poplar body and two single coil pickups

Les Paul Special-II E1: minimal decoration, bolt-on neck, all-mahogany body and two humbuckers

Les Paul 100 E1: basically a Studio with a bolt-on neck

Les Paul Prophecy: Fishman Fluence pickups, locking tuners and 24 frets

Les Paul Modern: contoured neck heel, locking tuners and asymmetrical slim neck profile

Les Paul Muse: chambered body, high-output pickups, metallic finished

Les Paul Tenor Ukulele: an acoustic ukulele shaped like a Les Paul

1959 Les Paul Standard: created by the Custom Shop with vintage-correct build and USA pickups

Epiphone – Artist Models

Joe Bonamassa Lazarus: inspired by Joe Bonamassa's '59 Burst

Alex Lifeson Les Paul Axcess Standard: contoured neck heel, Floyd Rose, piezo pickup for the Rush guitarist

Slash Victoria: Gold Top, Alnico 2 pickups

Slash Appetite: Appetite Burst, Alnico 2 pickups

Billie Joe Armstrong Les Paul Junior: mid-fifties style Junior for the Green Day frontman

Tommy Thayer Les Paul: Blue Sparkle Standard with chrome hardware and Seymour Duncan pickups for the Kiss solo guitarist

Vivian Campbell "Holy Diver" Les Paul: inspired by the black Standard played by Vivian Campbell on Dio's *Holy Diver* album, with DiMarzio X2N pickups and a brass nut

Jared James Nichols "Old Glory" Les Paul: 1954-style Custom with only a bridge P90, a Gold finish and a wraparound

Jerry Cantrell "Wino" Les Paul Custom: Wine-red maple top Custom with two humbuckers, one covered and the bridge pickup exposed for the Alice In Chains frontman

Jerry Cantrell Les Paul Custom Prophecy: Fishman Fluence pickups, locking tuners, 24 frets, Cantrell neck profile and neck inlays

Matt Heafy Les Paul Custom Origins: six or seven string Custom with two Fishman Fluence pickups and locking tuners for the Trivium frontman

GIBSON CUSTOM SHOP

1954 Les Paul Gold Top: reissue of the wraparound Gold Top with P90s

1956 Les Paul Gold Top: reissue of the Tune-o-matic Gold Top with P90s

1957 Les Paul Gold Top: reissue of the Tune-o-matic Gold Top with humbuckers

1958 Les Paul Standard: narrow frets, chunky neck, plain top

1959 Les Paul Standard: medium-jumbo frets, medium neck, figured top

1960 Les Paul Standard: medium-jumbo frets, slim neck, figured top

60th Anniversary 1960 Les Paul Standard: three versions (V1, V2 and V3) of the 1960 Burst based on different periods of the year during which they were made

1957 Les Paul Custom: all mahogany, available with two or three pickups and with three pickups + a Bigsby

1968 Les Paul Custom: maple top, two pickups, witch hat knobs

1968 Les Paul Standard Gold Top: reissue of a Gold Top from the very first batch of reissues that had a crown inlay on the headstock

1957 Les Paul Junior: single-cut Junior

1958 Les Paul Junior Double Cut: double-cut Junior

1957 Les Paul Special Single Cut: single-cut Special

1960 Les Paul Special Double Cut: double-cut Special

Les Paul Axcess Standard: slim neck with contoured heel, Floyd Rose, figured top

Les Paul Axcess Custom: the Black Beauty version of the Axcess

Les Paul Axcess Custom Figured Top: Custom specs with a figured top and Axcess neck

Les Paul Special Double-Cut Figured Top: 1960 double-cut Special with a figured maple top, a body binding, two humbuckers and a Tune-o-matic bridge

Les Paul Custom with Ebony Fingerboard: 1968-style Custom with weight relief

Gibson Custom Shop - Artist Models

Jerry Cantrell "Wino" Les Paul Custom: weight-relieved Wine-red Custom with Aged finish and uncovered bridge pickup

Mike Ness 1976 Les Paul Deluxe: replica of the Social Distortion guitarist's Gold Top Deluxe with sandwich body and P90s

Adam Jones 1979 V2 Les Paul Custom: replica of the Tool guitarist's 1979 Silverburst Custom

Sergio Vallin 1955 Les Paul Gold Top: replica of the Mana guitarist's 1955 Gold Top with a Bigsby and a bridge humbucker

GIBSON USA

Original - Les Paul Standard '50s: late-fifties style Standard with two humbuckers

Original - Les Paul Standard '50s-P90: early-fifties style Standard with two P90s

Original - Les Paul Standard '60s: 1960-style Standard with slim neck

Original - Les Paul Standard '70s Deluxe: late-fifties style Standard with two mini-humbuckers

Original - Les Paul Special: mid-fifties-style Special

Original - Les Paul Junior: mid-fifties-style Junior

Modern - Les Paul Modern: asymmetrical neck profile with contoured neck heel and ebony fingerboard, locking tuners, no poker chip, four push-pull pots

Modern - Les Paul Classic: 1960-style Standard with slim neck, exposed zebra pickups and four push-pull pots

Modern - Les Paul Studio: no binding, two pickups, slim neck and two push-pull pots

Modern - Les Paul Tribute: a vintage-oriented Studio with a rounder neck, no push-pull pots and vintage sunburst finishes

Modern - Les Paul Special Tribute-P90: single-cut Special

Modern - Les Paul Special Tribute-humbucker: single-cut Special with two exposed humbuckers

GIBSON
LES PAUL DC
PRO (NINETIES
VERSION)

NEW MODEL NO. 15

GIBSON
LES PAUL DARK
FIRE

The Les Paul Model was released in 1952, so it was only logical that Gibson would keep on trying new ways to improve on the original design, or at least new styles that would appeal to different customers. The Les Paul DC Pro came out in 1997. The idea was simple: DC stood for "double cutaway", and it took the dual-cut-away shape of the late-fifties Les Paul Junior and Special but applied it a Les Paul Standard, i.e. with a maple top and crown inlays. This design had been an underground favorite for decades for the easy access it gave to the upper frets and for its very different visual vibe, perhaps less inextricably linked with Jimmy Page and seventies hard rock. Pat Travers, Joan Jett and French guitarist Nono from Trust have all been touring for years with modified double-cutaway Melody Makers featuring two humbuckers, and guitar builder Paul Reed Smith has based the P.R.S. brand identity on double-cutaway guitars that share a lot of DNA with the Les Paul Standard, including flamed maple tops and dual humbuckers.

The truss rod cover on the headstock of the ES-Les Paul has a picture of an F-hole.

It was only logical that Gibson would retaliate and come up with their own version of the DC, but the DC Pro had a strange, narrow headstock unlike any classic Gibson model, also used on the first ES-336 of that era. The logo barely seemed to fit on top of it, and it was not a visual success, especially with the dot inlays on the neck that did not give the DC Pro the overall vibe of a luxury instrument. Fortunately, Gibson has released many other versions of the DC, including models sharing the same visual appointments as the Gold Top or Black Beauty Custom. They remain a fun alternative but have yet to really make their mark on the guitar world.

Another concept that appeared in the nineties but really hit its stride a few years later was to make a semi-hollow Les Paul. Gibson invented the semi-hollow electric guitar in 1958 with the ES-335, which was the perfect meeting of a solid body and a fully hollow archtop. The ES-335 had a top glued on back and sides like an archtop, but it had a solid block of wood going through the body to prevent it from feedbacking. The concept was obviously a success (and continues to be a lasting classic to this day), but strangely it has not been turned into a proper Les Paul-derived model until the Custom Shop Les Paul Bantam in 1995. One year later, Washburn claimed the name Bantam which they had been using for their models, so it became the Les Paul Florentine. It looked like a fancy Custom with figured maple, gold hardware

GIBSON
ES-LES PAUL 2015

GIBSON
LES PAUL
SUPREME 2003

The back is just as
flamed as the top, and
the headstock inlay
can only be found on
that model.

and the split diamond on the headstock, but it had two f-holes on either side of the body. Not only was this a beautiful new version of a familiar instrument, but it was also a nice way of relieving the weight with the semi-hollow structure. Customers had been very divided on the idea of chambered Les Paul bodies, but on the Florentine it made sense from the get-go. The difference in sound was not colossal, which might account for the model's limited success. It became the ES-Les Paul in 2014 to make things even clearer, and to distinguish it from the guitars built in the Custom Shop, since this one was built at the Memphis factory, where all the semi-hollow body guitars were made until 2017. That version has been released under many forms, some of them quite experimental and others very close to the historic classics, some luxurious and others more stripped-down. In 2016, it even became a signature model for Canadian prog-rock legend Alex Lifeson of the band Rush: his version was a white Custom with two f-holes. Lifeson was no stranger to championing leftfield variations on the Les Paul theme, since he had already released a signature Axcess in 2011. The Axcess was the evolution of eighties Les Pauls being modded with a Floyd-Rose. It was a Gibson-made Les Paul with a factory Floyd Rose and a contoured neck heel for better access to the highest frets.

In 2003, the Les Paul Supreme became the absolute top of the regular USA-made line, trying to out-Custom the Custom with flamed top and back (with a heavy flame on the back like on an archtop guitar) around a chambered mahogany body, with Custom bindings and gold hardware and Super-400 split inlays. To this day, the Supreme is the guitar that Gibson employees receive as a gift when they've been working at the company for twenty years.

Finally, one of the most interesting Les Pauls of the noughties was released in 2006, under the decidedly un-poetic name HD.6X-Pro. It was a light blue silverburst Les Paul with strange tuners, but the real magic was an hexaphonic pickup that would send a separate signal for each string to a breakout box, giving the possibility of processing each string differently. This was the first foray of the Les Paul into the digital world, and the symbolic link with Lester Polfuss'

early experiments was not lost on Gibson, who released a limited edition of 100 HD.6X-Pro signed by Les.

One year later, in 2007, Gibson released the Robot Guitar, with a variation on the same finish but another digital feature that made it an instant hit: a self-tuning system. In the late eighties, a company called TransPerformance had developed a bridge that would allow the player to switch from one tuning to another, which was used by open-tuning enthusiasts Sonny Landreth and Jimmy Page (both on Les Pauls). But the Robot Guitar's system was less invasive and could tune your guitar up in mere seconds: needless to say, it became an instant hit and several non-limited versions have followed.

Following that success, Gibson must have thought that the sky was the limit, so in 2008 they came up with the Dark Fire, a Les Paul with a red flame top, black hardware and binding, a neck P90 and the traditional L-5 flower pot on the headstock. It brought together the hexaphonic pickup possibilities of the HD.6X-Pro along with the self-tuning of the Robot, as well as new features like many available pickup combinations. Unfortunately, the Dark Fire had been hastily designed and the self-tuning system did not work as it should have. The guitar marked the end of the first run of digital Les Pauls.

Even though all of these models were interesting extrapolations in their own right, the Les Paul market has always been artist-driven, and since the new models were not picked as the main axe of rock stars of the age, they have mostly remained nice curiosities. In 2009 for instance, the Gibson catalog had the Billie Joe Armstrong Junior (the Green Day singer had been a fan of the Junior since their smash hit *American Idiot* in 2004), the Gary Moore BFG (for Barely Finished Guitar, basically a cheap Standard with a raw finish, a P90 at the neck and no poker chip), and Custom Shop guitars inspired by Steve Jones, Warren Haynes (Gov't Mule guitarist and singer), Peter Frampton, Slash, Zakk Wylde, Joe Bonamassa, Mick Jones (of Foreigner, not to be mistaken for Mick Jones of The Clash who also loved his Customs and double-cut Juniors), Jeff Beck and Mike Bloomfield.

GIBSON
GARY MOORE
SIGNATURE
LES PAUL BFG

GIBSON
LES PAUL ROBOT

BONAMASSA GALORE

Joe Bonamassa performing at Shepherds Bush Empire on 30th December 2010 in London.

Among the many signature models that made the backbone and most visible part of the Gibson catalog in the noughties, Joe Bonamassa's name reigns supreme. Bonamassa was a child-prodigy who was mentored by Telecaster-master Danny Gatton at age 11, started touring professionally and spent a tour opening for B.B. King at age 12. His real popular breakthrough came with the album *You & Me* in 2006 when he started working with producer Kevin Shirley (Iron Maiden, The Black Crowes, Rush). Since then, he has released an average one album a year, alternating between studio and live records, and has been performing more than seventy shows per year.

But most importantly for the topic at hand, Bonamassa's father was a music store owner, and Joe got the collecting and vintage bugs very early on. He bought his first Burst in 2010 and has not been shy about using it on tour. In fact, he called that guitar Magellan after the 16th-century navigator as a reference to the fact that he's been playing that Burst all around the world. Before him, very few players would actually dare to take a Burst out on the road, mostly arena acts such as Paul McCartney (who plays an even rarer left-handed 1960 Burst), Peter Frampton, Steve Miller or producer John Shanks with Bon Jovi. But over the years, Bonamassa has acquired an insane collection of impossibly rare vintage pieces, including a grand total of 15 Bursts (and a few others he sold along the way), and he has never shied away from taking them on the tour bus. That attitude has reinforced the Burst mystique, making it current and even more fascinating now that it was being not only collected with love, but also played live every night. All of Joe's Bursts have a name, and his most hardcore fans will recognize them at first glance. Joe also happens to be a great storyteller and has worked hard on his online presence; as a result all his guitars are well-known and much talked-about, and keep the myth of the untouched-Les-Paul-tucked-under-the-bed-for-forty-years intact and vibrant: these crazy stories have happened to Bonamassa, so they could happen to any of us.

Perhaps contrary to expectations, Bonamassa has made the choice to concentrate on Epiphone signatures rather than steep-priced Custom Shop limited editions. It started that way with the Gold Top "Inspired By" Joe Bonamassa (a designation that has replaced the "signature" moniker for most artist models in the Gibson

JOE BONAMASSA

BEACON THEATRE: LIVE
FROM NEW YORK

2012

catalog) in 2008, a beautiful 1957-style Standard with black pickup rings and pickguard. But in 2011 he released a much cheaper Studio version. Overall, he has designed seven Gibson signature models, including a Burst replica (the Skinner Burst in 2014), and the weirdly gorgeous Bonabyrd in 2015, an Antique Pelham Blue Les Paul with humbuckers, a wraparound bridge and a Firebird six-in-line headstock (hence the "bird" part of the name, with a Y as a reference to the classic Gibson Byrdland released in 1955).

But to this day, Bonamassa has released no fewer than nine Epiphone models, most of them "story" models, i.e. replicas of insanely rare Gibsons that are only available under that cheaper brand – not just lesser versions of high-end Custom Shop guitars. The most recent three are the Norm Burst in 2019 (a 1960 Burst), the Black Beauty in 2020 (a three-pickup 1958 Custom) and Lazarus in 2021 (a 1959 Burst that had been painted red and brought to its former glory by Bonamassa). All of these have been limited editions whose prices are really taking off on the used market, which would have been hard to imagine for Epiphone-branded Les Pauls only a few years ago, and which also raises the question of what is a reissue and whether it really makes any sense to try and copy those guitars of yesteryear.

**GIBSON
CUSTOM SHOP**

JOE BONAMASSA
BONABYRD 2015

**GIBSON
CUSTOM SHOP**

JOE BONAMASSA
"SKINNERBURST" 59
LES PAUL STANDARD
2014

GIBSON

JOE BONAMASSA
LES PAUL STUDIO
GOLD TOP 2011

EPIPHONE

JOE BONAMASSA
BLACK BEAUTY
LES PAUL CUSTOM
OUTFIT 2020

THE REISSUE PARADOX

1993 Gibson ad for
The Historic Collection
featuring a '39 reissue
Super 400 and a
'59 reissue Les Paul
Flametop.

The actual Historic reissues by the Custom Shop began in 1994, after which previous reissues have been nicknamed "Pre-Historic". Those beautiful flame-top Bursts were a significant step up compared with previous attempts, yet they would keep on evolving over time.

The trend begs the question: were the reissues a doomed enterprise from the start? When players say they want an accurate reissue of a fifties Les Paul, what do they exactly mean? And can it even be done? Fifties Les Pauls were made by hand, one at a time, without much thought given to consistency. The logos wouldn't always be in the same spot on the headstock, neck shapes would vary, the carving of the top can be day and night from one guitar to the next, and the maple tops on Bursts can have very different patterns. Gibson wouldn't charge extra for a flamed top or double white pickups, you would get what you would get. Modern customers expect more from their purchase: they want to know exactly what they are paying for, and by definition it becomes a strange proposition to design a predictable reissue of an unpredictable guitar.

Not two original Bursts are alike, so Gibson had to struggle to define the "ideal" vintage Les Paul, the platonic form of a Burst, the unchanging idea among the impermanent representations. Ideal specs are always hard to define: do players really want the thinner frets on the '58? Do they want the super low frets of the original Black Beauty on their Custom reissue? Or the all-mahogany body on that Custom? Or unpotted pickups like the original PAFs that will be prone to feedback? Low-output trebly PAFs

Following in the
footsteps of stores
custom-ordering their
Burst replicas in the
seventies, Rumble
Seat Music (Nashville,
Tennessee) has
worked closely with
the Custom Shop to
create their own '59
reissue in 2018. This is
the first prototype for
that run.

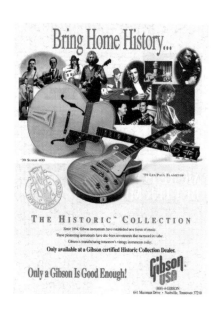

or fatter-sounding modern humbuckers that will probably sound better if you're not playing on a 100-watt Marshall stack?

By definition, living up to the expectations of every player is impossible, since each one of us has their own idea of the perfect Burst. That idea mostly comes from listening to albums and staring at photos since many of us have not been lucky enough to spend some time playing the real deal. Reissues have been a long time coming, and they still represent a struggle to this day. They have become the bread and butter of the Custom Shop line, and have turned into their own style of instruments. Most of us have not even seen an actual Burst in person, and if we played one it might not live up to what we would want it to be: we have gotten used to the consistency and build quality of modern-day Gibsons. If we had to compare an actual Burst

**GIBSON
CUSTOM SHOP**
58 LES PAUL
STANDARD
REISSUE 2013

**GIBSON
CUSTOM SHOP**

TRUE HISTORIC
60 LES PAUL
STANDARD
REISSUE 2015

As opposed to vintage guitars, you can choose your sunburst on a reissue, from the dark Tobacco Burst on the '58 to the Lemon Burst on the '60.

and a good modern replica blindfolded, a lot of us would likely go for the replica.

Burst reissues have become their own style of instruments, almost independent from the originals. Given the price of an original on the current vintage market, it would be quite hypocritical to pretend those are still musical instruments: they are investments, meant to be stored away and handled with kid gloves. The real instruments are the reissues. Gibson built the original Burst for just three years, while they have been making Burst reissues for over forty years and counting, so it's safe to say that by now they have gotten it right, with ideal specs that have even retroactively changed our perception of vintage Bursts to a point. The R8 (R for Reissue, 8 for 1958) has a plain top and a big neck, the R9 has flame and the perfect not-too-small-not-too-big neck, and the R0 has a slim neck, flame and reflector knobs. Of course, the originals didn't work like that, and each one of them was its own thing.

For a while, Gibson had embraced that original chaos with the Collector's Choice series. These claimed to be exact replicas of one vintage

LES PAUL

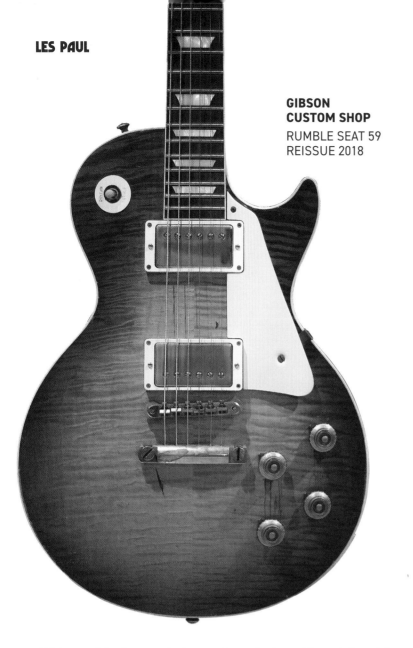

GIBSON CUSTOM SHOP
RUMBLE SEAT 59 REISSUE 2018

This is one of the five production models from the Rumble Seat Reissue run.

Someone asked for this '54 Oxblood reissue as part of the Made To Measure program. It is safe to assume they must have been quite fond of Jeff Beck.

highly individual guitars (they were only made in small runs, each number with its own personal specs).

Of course, since the whole raison d'être for the reissues is to be as close to the original as possible, every new discovery on the originals allows the reissues to get even closer. Every time Gibson's R&D department gets their hands on a Burst they haven't seen before, and gets to digitally scan it, they are able to incorporate what they have found into their production.

That new process really took off in 2004 with the Jimmy Page Number One replica, for which the Custom Shop team flew over to England, met Page and digitally scanned the guitar, taking every possible measurement in order to make the most faithful replica that could be made. The neck was especially tricky, since the original had been sanded down so it did not look like a typical Burst neck at all. Since then, the Custom Shop has scanned hundreds of vintage guitars so they could find the ideal middle ground between all those individual specs.

The problem with that process is that the buying public will eventually get tired of reading about the new reissues that are supposedly even closer than previous reissues, which were supposed to be as close as it gets at the time, and so on. This can even trigger delayed buyer's remorse when the new reissues come out and that previous reissue becomes last year's model.

This is what happened in 2015 when Gibson released the True Historic series: those Custom Shop guitars were supposed to be the most exact replicas they had ever built, and they were really wonderful, faithful instruments indeed. The problem is that the Custom Shop was still building "regular" reissues, the R series and then the CS series. Obviously, since those were priced a little cheaper and they weren't backed by the same marketing hype as the True Historics, they were perceived as a lower-grade option for reissue enthusiasts, which ultimately can only be detrimental to the whole line. Since there were True Historics, to some of us it could only mean that the rest of them were "Fake Historics"! Gibson has been smart enough not to keep that distinction after 2017.

instrument in particular, quirks and all, and since they were limited editions they didn't have to correspond to everyone's notion of an ideal Burst. Gibson would usually make about 300 guitars of each number, starting out in 2010 with CC#01, the "Melvyn Franks Les Paul", named after the owner of the Peter Green/Gary Moore Burst at the time. A fitting start to a great series that stopped in 2017 after 47 limited runs, including a few non-Bursts like Tom Sholz's 1968 stripped Gold Top, two Gold Tops, a Junior, a Custom, an ES-335 and even a Firebird. But the rest of them were Bursts, either famous ones or lesser-known guitars with cool stories. Nowadays, the Collector's Choice series are increasing in value on the used market since they reconcile the two contradictory features that most collectors are looking for: they are predictable (each number corresponds to a particular model with well-defined specs) yet

LIKE YOUR FAVORITE PAIR OF JEANS

The Custom Shop creates both extravagantly high-end instruments like this none-more-gold 50th Anniversary Custom, and guitars that look as though they've been carefully played for a few decades, like the '60 Aged reissue.

From the time when it became a fully grown structure in 1994, the Custom Shop had to fulfill two tasks at the same time: on the one hand, they were in charge of custom orders, what would later become the "Made To Measure" (or M2M) program, meaning they were supposed to be able to build anything customers would want, usually within the confines of what was in line with the brand identity (they would probably not accept an order for a Telecaster, for instance). Those M2M customers could be collectors looking for that elusive shade of Burst they've been after, budding musicians looking for their ultimate tool or pro superstars gearing up with fun colorful stuff for their next world tour.

On the other hand, they were building reissues and their goal was to make them as close as possible to the great old ones. Tom Murphy has been really instrumental in that evolution. He started at Gibson in 1989 in the finish repair department, then moved on to the Custom Shop, and as a true stickler for details he presented a very precise list of fine points to concentrate on in order to get the reissues absolutely right. The fact that '90s reissues suddenly got so much better compared with their '80s counterparts is almost entirely Murphy's work. He left the company in 1994 to create Guitar Preservation, but he was still freelancing for Gibson at the same time.

In 1995, Fender came up with the Relics, Custom Shop vintage replicas that had been aged at the factory by artist Vince Cunetto. Today, we take pre-aged guitars for granted, but Fender was a real trailblazer at that point, so much so that "relic" or "relicing" have become part of the guitar lingo without necessarily being applied to the California brand anymore.

Tom Murphy was Gibson's answer to Vince Cunetto, but he had to design a way of aging Les Pauls from the ground up, since Fender's tricks would not really work for a Gibson. As previously mentioned, the Les Paul is a delicate and refined instrument, with a few highly sensitive areas (the neck joint, the headstock) that should not be weakened by aging. Les Pauls are not paddles, they are not planks, they have set necks that break easily, and cannot be bashed in the same way as a Telecaster. As it ages, the finish of a Les Paul creates patterns that are extremely tricky to replicate, but Murphy was up to the task, and in 1999 Gibson introduced the Standard 1959 Aged. Since then, most aged Les Pauls have been done by Murphy himself, or by someone else using Murphy's methods. It is easy to tell a Murphy from a non-Murphy aged since the former has the TM letters engraved below the bridge volume knob as part of the aging.

Why would a player or collector be looking for a pre-aged guitar? It is not by sheer chance that aged finishes became part of the discussion

Those two SGs (Pelham Blue Standard and Polaris White Special) are from the Murphy Lab and have been aged in a very believable way.

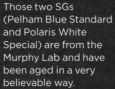

GIBSON

CUSTOM SHOP 50TH ANNIVERSARY LES PAUL CUSTOM 2007

GIBSON

CUSTOM SHOP 60 LES PAUL STANDARD REISSUE AGED 2012

**GIBSON
MURPHY LAB**

LES PAUL JUNIOR
'60 ULTRA HEAVY
AGED

in the late nineties: this is the point when the vintage market started going out of control, with prices for a nice fifties Les Paul truly skyrocketing. Just like that, most buyers were priced out of even a good Gold Top, so they turned to the Custom Shop – but they still wanted the status and romanticism of an old, beat-up instrument, one that has earned its battle scars on countless stages throughout the years. The good Bursts are good because they have been played, much more than any particular build quality of the fifties that would be impossible to replicate. Therefore, the truly beat-up ones are the most appealing to the players in-the-know. Astute collector Joe Bonamassa puts it bluntly: "The ones that are museum pieces are normally the ones that are shit. No one's ever wanted them. The ones that were beat up and completely trashed are the ones everyone plays, because they were and are the best."

In 2006, the Custom Shop introduced VOS (for Vintage Original Specs), which is both a series of "standard" reissues (an original set of 17 including the three years of the Burst, the '57 single-cut Junior, the '58 double-cut Junior, the 1961 SG – technically a Les Paul – and others) and also a minimum level of aging that is standard on most reissues. VOS means the instrument has no dings, but the finish doesn't shine like a new guitar would, and the hardware parts are slightly patinated. This process gives a vintage feel to brand new instruments, and prevents the reissues from being too glossy and shiny.

Finally, in 2021, Gibson introduced the Murphy Lab, a department of the Custom Shop that offers four gradual levels of aging, from Ultra Light to Ultra Heavy. This allows an unprecedented predictability when you're ordering your own made-to-measure Les Paul. The Murphy method has evolved over time, to the point that he now uses a special lacquer that ages much more quickly, instead of adding a patina on top of the finish of a regular Custom Shop instrument. As the price of vintage Les Pauls keeps on going up, the Murphy Lab should not be running out of orders anytime soon.

The TM (for Tom Murphy) signature in the aging has been made obvious on the second picture.

GIBSON CUSTOM SHOP
LES PAUL CUSTOM M2M

M2M by definition : a Custom with a pirate skull at the 5th fret, black hardware and an ultra-figured top from the Gibson Vault.

COLLECTOR'S CHOICES

This is the complete list of Collector's Choice models to the best of our knowledge. That famous series is quite hard to follow since they did not necessarily come out in a chronological fashion. Since the series came to a halt in 2017, some numbers have not been attributed, leaving a few gaps.

Only two models (#42 and #47) are not Les Pauls,
and among the Les Pauls the overwhelming majority are '59 Bursts.
Out of 39 models, there are twenty-two 1959s, six 1960s and three 1958s.

CC#01: Melvyn Franks (2010)
This is the '59 Burst that belonged to Peter Green, then Gary Moore. When that replica was released it had not been bought by Kirk Hammett yet.

CC#02: Goldie (2011)
A gorgeous lemon-burst '59 that has belonged to several collectors.

CC#03: The Babe (2012)
This 1960 Bigsby-equipped Cherry Burst belonged to Joe Bonamassa, who nicknamed it "The Batman" because the shape of the plaque under the tune-o-matic looks like the famous Batman logo. For copyright reasons, the nickname has been changed to "The Babe".

CC#04: Sandy (2012)
A Dirty Lemon Burst '59 with exposed zebra pickups.

CC#05: Donna (2015)
A darker-sunburst '59 that belongs to author Tom Wittrock. Like most Collector's Choice from 2015 on, this was built with True Historic specs, and came out three years after number 4.

CC#06: Number One (2012)
This darker-burst '59 is the favorite of collector Mike Slubowski, who also happens to be the president of Trinity Health, a major US health system.

CC#07: John Shanks (2013)
A bright-red '60 with Grover tuners. The original belongs to Bon Jovi guitarist and producer John Shanks.

CC#08: The Beast (2013)
This stunning Lemon Burst '59 belongs to Bernie Mardsen of Whitesnake.

CC#09: The Believer Burst (2013)
This highly-figured '59 Cherry Burst belongs to collector Vic DaPra who used it for the cover of his book *Burst Believers*, hence the name.

CC#10: Tom Scholz (2013)
This is a replica of the famous guitar used by Tom Scholz, the mastermind behind the band Boston, for every guitar track on the 1981 self-titled debut of the band that include the hit single "More Than A Feeling". It was a 1968 Gold Top P90-equipped reissue, which Scholz stripped down to a natural finish and modified with a bridge humbucker and Grovers.

CC#11: Rosie (2013)
A '59 with a Red burst that has remained really dark and vibrant overtime.

CC#12: Henry Goldtop (2014)
A '57 Gold Top owned by Gibson CEO Henry Juszkiewicz.

CC#13: The Spoonful Burst (2014)
This Dirty Lemon Burst '59 was John Sebastian's main guitar for most of his career in the Lovin' Spoonful and solo.

COLLECTOR'S CHOICES

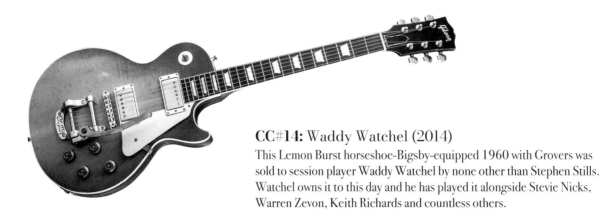

CC#14: Waddy Watchel (2014)

This Lemon Burst horseshoe-Bigsby-equipped 1960 with Grovers was sold to session player Waddy Watchel by none other than Stephen Stills. Watchel owns it to this day and he has played it alongside Stevie Nicks, Warren Zevon, Keith Richards and countless others.

CC#15: Greg Martin (2014)

This is the first '58 of the series, a beautiful Faded Dirty Lemon Burst owned and played by Greg Martin of the band Kentucky Headhunters.

CC#16: Red Eye (2014)

This '59 belonged to Lynyrd Skynyrd guitarist Ed King, and its name comes from the red spot next to the pickup switch.

CC#17: Louis (2014)

This Faded Lemon Burst '59 belongs to Buckcherry guitarist Keith Nelson.

CC#18: The Dutchburst (2014)

That Dark Burst '60 belonged to a Dutch jazz guitarist, and it ended up being sold by Max Guitar in the Netherlands decades later.

CC#24: Nicky (2015)

This is a '59 Burst that belongs to collector Charles Daughtry.

CC#26: The Whitford Burst (2014)

A '59 belonging to Aerosmith guitarist Brad Whitford.

CC#28: STP Burst (2014)

This '58 belonged to Ronnie Montrose.

CC#29: Tamio Okuda (2015)

This '59 belongs to Japanese rock star Tamio Okuda.

CC#30: Gabby (2014)

A one-owner '59 with a vibrant Cherry sunburst bought by Vic DaPra.

CC#19: Dave Hinson (2016)

And now for something completely different: this is a '59 black double-cutaway Les Paul Junior.

CC#22: Tommy Colletti (2015)

Colletti is the owner of the guitar store The Music Zoo, and he bought this beautiful '59 Black Beauty with three pickups from James Honeyman-Scott, the original guitarist and founder of The Pretenders.

CC#31: Mike Reeder/The Snake (2015)

Mike Reeder is the owner of Mike's Music in Cincinnati, Ohio. This '59 is the finest Les Paul in his collection.

CC#33: Jeff Hanna (2015)

This stunning '60 belongs to Jeff Hanna from the Nitty Gritty Dirt Band.

CC#34: The Blackburst (2015)

That one started its life as a 1960 Burst, but a customer ordered a black Standard since he could not afford a Custom. The Gibson workers painted it black over the original sunburst, hence the name Blackburst. The Custom Shop did the exact same thing for that run, and they even included a photograph of the original sunburst finish with the guitar.

COLLECTOR'S CHOICES

CC#35: Gruhn Burst (2016)

George Gruhn is a legend in the vintage guitar world, both as a writer and store owner. He sold this spectacular '59 Burst to Vic DaPra back in the eighties.

CC#36: Goldfinger (2016)

This is a '57 Gold Top that belongs to collector Charles Daughtry.

CC#37: Carmelita (2016)

A '59 Burst with a highly-figured top.

CC#38: Chicken Shack (2017)

A '60 Burst with exposed double-white pickups. It belonged to Stan Webb of the band Chicken Shack.

CC#39: Minnesota Burst (2016)

A flamed '59 Burst sold to a store in Minnesota by the original owner, currently owned by UK collector Andrew Raymond.

CC#42: JD Simo (2016)

This is by far the shortest run of the series with only 25 guitars made, and the most unexpected of the lot, since this is a semi-hollow Cherry Red ES-335. The 1962 original belongs to Nashville guitar-slinger extraordinaire J.D. Simo.

CC#43: Mick Ralphs (2017)

This '58 Burst belonged to Mick Ralphs, singer, guitarist and founder of the bands Mott The Hoople and Bad Company.

CC#44: Happy Jack (2017)

This gorgeous '59 with double whites was bought new by a member of the Tommy Dorsey Orchestra, then sold to an Ohio musician named Jack (hence the name), then bought by collector Vic DaPra.

CC#45: Danger Burst (2016)

A Lemon Burst '59 with heavy flaming.

CC#46: Kathryn (2017)

This Cherry Burst '59 belongs to musician Scott Bradoka.

CC#47: Firebird III (2017)

The only other non-Les Paul of the series, and the last one released. This is a very cool reverse Firebird III (two pickups, dot inlays, short vibrola) in a very rare Cherry Red finish.

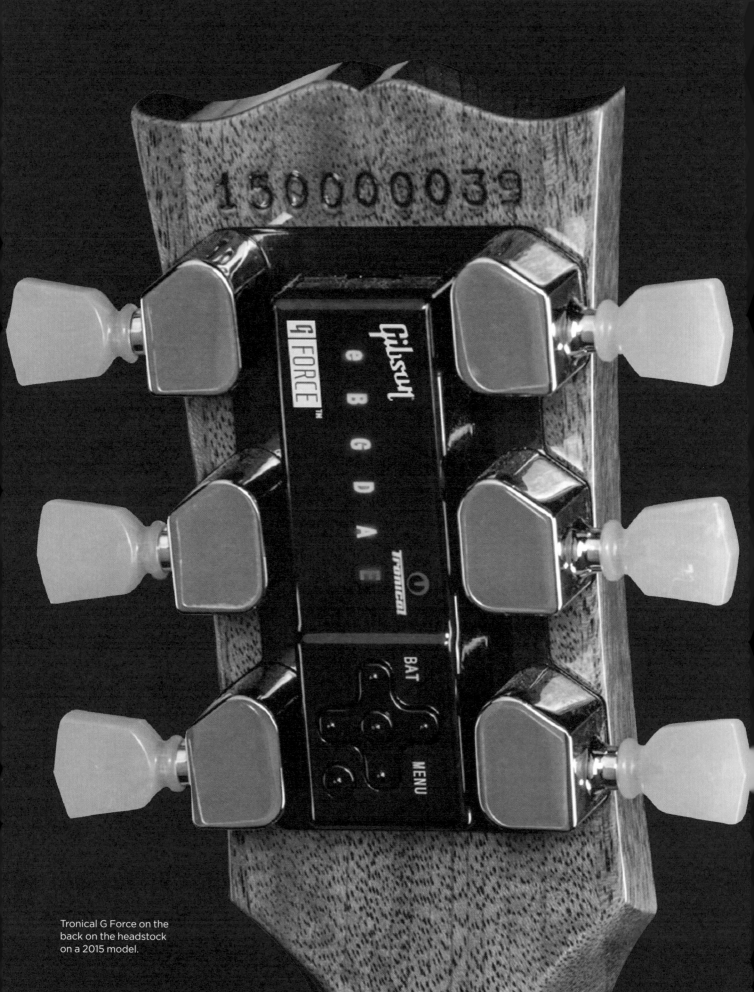

Tronical G Force on the
back on the headstock
on a 2015 model.

MEET THE NEW BOSS

The Murphy Lab is part of many new ideas that have been implemented by the new Gibson regime that took over in 2019. But getting there has been incredibly challenging for the employees, the stores and even the customers. The 2010s was a very dark decade for Gibson, some of which was visible from the outside but most of which was not.

In November 2009, federal agents raided the Nashville plant and seized imported ebony. In August 2011, another raid took place, both in Nashville and Memphis, this time to seize Indian rosewood, and Gibson agreed to pay penalties and make sizeable environmental donations.

During that same year, Gibson acquired the Stanton Group (including audio brands like KRK and Stanton DJ) and formed the Gibson Pro Audio division. There were other buyouts, which culminated in April 2014 when Gibson bought the audio, video and multimedia part of Phillips. That buyout was apparently more than Gibson could financially chew, and Henry Juszkiewicz's vision of turning Gibson into a major music lifestyle group was never fully realized, instead leading to the brand's demise.

From a guitar point of view, Gibson's *annus horribilis* was 2015. The seeds had already been planted in 2013, when the mention "2013 Model" started to appear on the back of USA guitars. Henry Juszkiewicz wanted to present a full new line of guitars every year, just like car brands do, in order to keep the market interested. But car brands introduce new technologies that justify a yearly new model, and customers expect those updates. Nobody would dream of taking

a car from the sixties with its original motor on a freeway, whereas most guitarists would gladly take a 1960 Les Paul over any new thing Gibson could come up with. The two markets are not alike.

The yearly line for 2015 was designed in a single meeting. All new features were mandated by the direction, and employees were requested to go along with it. Three major innovations define that year: self-tuning tuners, an adjustable brass nut and a wider neck. The tuners were an evolution of the German system Tronical Min-Etune, close to what was on the Dusk Tiger. That system became available as an option in 2012, but in 2015 it was renamed G Force and put on every single USA model. There were three major issues with that decision: firstly, the product itself was not perfectly reliable. As Mat Koehler, now senior director of product development, says: "the technology wasn't fully-baked, it wasn't stage-tested. It was more of a putting out fires mentality more than a long term strategy". Koehler even confesses that in 2016, since the stores had not sold a large part of their 2015 inventory, "we've literally had to go to stores and replace the tuners". Secondly, the G Force was forced onto players. It was not an option, and you could not request your Gibson

GIBSON
LES PAUL
STANDARD 2015

James "J.C." Curleigh making a speech during the Gibson NAMM Jam in 2019.

without it. Lastly, there was an innate contradiction between the durable and heritage image of Gibson and this new digital gizmo seemingly slapped on it. People usually buy a Gibson – which are expensive instruments – because they know they are lasting objects that they will keep for a lifetime and hopefully pass on to their kids. A G Force system, as a digital consumer product, has a limited lifespan. The juxtaposition of the two was especially shocking on a model like the Les Paul Traditional, a high-end Burst-like USA instrument.

The brass nut was not necessarily a bad idea. It had originally been designed as a substitute for the zero fret Tony Iommi wanted on his signature model, but the call was made to put it on every single model that year. Again, this is where things went south: Gibson had a very

large catalog of guitars, yet customers did not really have a say on the features they wanted.

The wider neck was designed as a reaction to customers complaining that frets would hit the binding on previous models. But the cure turned out to be worse than the sickness, as master luthier Jim DeCola explains: "The idea was, 'Let's make the neck wider and keep the string spacing the same, that way you have more fret on each side.' Henry said 0.050 inch per side, and I thought he meant 0.015, but he actually said 0.050, and I thought, 'Oh my god, that's way too much!'"

And, of course, since he was in charge of doing promo videos for the new line, DeCola became the proverbial bearer of bad news, and the fact that he had managed to include true mother of pearl inlays on the 2015 models quickly became drowned out by the noise of customer complaints: "I'm the one who has to do the video and tell people about it, I was the messenger, and a lot of people blamed me for that. That was a very uncomfortable year for myself personally, and for the company. It cost a lot of damage to our reputation and sales."

But the USA line wasn't the only one that suffered. Like a Shakespearean king who falls deeper into madness as the state of his kingdom gets worse, those at the top were persisting with ideas of turning Gibson into a lifestyle company of the future rather than accepting it as a heritage brand. This is why in 2017 it was decided that a new product had to be launched every single week, in order to keep both employees and customers on their toes. On top of this, the Custom Shop was asked to stop doing reissues and instead concentrate on designing new products. Following those decisions, the situation kept deteriorating until the 1st of May 2018, when Gibson had to file for Chapter 11 bankruptcy protection. During the bankruptcy process, the difficult times did not stop, quite the opposite: at the Custom Shop, 18 of the older more experienced employees were fired in a single day. The process finally ended in October, and the decision was made that Gibson should focus on musical instruments. James "J.C." Curleigh, the former president of global brands at Levi Strauss, became the new CEO, and things started to change.

PLAY LIST

IN FLAMES
Trigger (2002)

METALLICA
Frantic (2003)

GREEN DAY
American Idiot (2004)

JOE BONAMASSA
Sloe Gin (2007)

RUSH
Clockwork Angels (2012)

TRIVIUM
Strife (2013)

RAMMSTEIN
Zeit (2022)

IT'S A NEW DAY

The Gibson Garage, complete with a few semi-hollow guitars on a conveyor belt.

A very unexpected duet: Les Paul (playing what appears to be a standard-sized sunburst Les Paul Professional with Bigsby) and Slash.

The 2019 Summer NAMM Show reintroduced Gibson with a newfound vigor and confidence, presenting completely revamped USA and Custom Shop lines, and a new trimmed-down catalog that's much easier to understand. During that same period, Gibson enlisted the help of Mark Agnesi, who had built a solid social media presence for the California vintage store Norman's Rare Guitars, and with his help Gibson TV has started producing very high-quality long-form videos on the likes of YouTube, on subjects ranging from classic albums, venues and studios to artists and their guitar collections.

In January 2021, Gibson bought the Mesa Boogie brand of amplifiers, a much more coherent and modest decision than the previous buyouts of the 2010s. At the time of writing, Gibson has not launched the renewed Mesa line, but it should finally give them a good line of well-made and esteemed amplifiers to match their guitars.

Later that same year, Gibson launched the Gibson Garage, a highly ambitious flagship store in the center of Nashville. The store combines a massive stock of every Gibson and Epiphone model available, as well as a Custom Shop department to help customers design their dream guitar, a stage for Gibson artists to perform on and a V.I.P. section that is host to some current models for artists to borrow in videos and photoshoots, but also to a small selection of the most desirable vintage Gibsons ever, including four Les Pauls.

Finally, in July of 2021, Gibson launched their own label, Gibson Records, and announced that Slash's next solo record would be their first release. The new regime has only been there for less than half a decade, but it feels like the brand has become exciting again, and they are yet to run out of cool ideas to get us guitar geeks excited.

Les Paul himself died in August 2009, so he never got to see the turmoils of the 2010 decade. Yet, he lived long enough to be perfectly conscious – and proud – of his incredible legacy. Gibson is the house that Les built: even today, Les Pauls make for about 80 per cent of the 420 guitars made every day at the Nashville plant. They rule supreme on the vintage market, and still represent the ultimate instrument for many players.

Just two months before Les Paul died, he played his last show at the Iridium, a jazz club in New York where he had been playing every Monday night for decades. That passion and that dedication to the craft have made the Les Paul what it is, and will continue to be: the Stradivarius of rock n' roll.

INDEX

A

Aerosmith 133, 140, 142, 155, 183, 188, 230
Agnesi (Mark) 236
Alice In Chains 195, 199, 201
Allman (Duane) 99, 136, 137, 142, 158, 188
Allman (Gregg) 136, 137
Allman Brothers Band (The) 136, 137, 139, 141, 155, 158
Armstrong (Jim) 201
Asheton (Ron) 153
Atkins (Chet) 16, 70
Atkins (Jimmy) 16

B

Bad Company 231
Baker (Mickey) 58, 67
Baldwin 116, 161
Ball (Lucille) 107
Band of Gypsys 109
Baranet (Max) 185
Barr (Holly) 136
Barre (Martin) 146
Basie (Count) 13
Bassey (Shirley) 95
Beatles (The) 89, 94, 107, 114, 127, 129, 146
Beato (John) 5
Beato (Rick) 5, 141
Beauchamp (George) 15
Beck (Jeff) 20, 97, 104, 105, 107, 108, 111, 114, 127, 142, 215, 222
Beecher (Franny) 58, 59
Benny Goodman Sextet (The) 25
Berlin (Maurice) 33, 116
Berry (Chuck) 59, 67, 92
Berryman (David) 180
Betts (Dickey) 137
Bigsby (Paul A.) 28, 29
Black Country Communion 216
Black Crowes (The) 216
Black Label Society 193
Black Sabbath 136, 190
Bloomfield (Mike) 108, 109, 111, 116, 133, 215
Blue Incorporated 92
Bluesbreakers (The) 94, 97, 99, 101, 104, 111
Bolan (Marc) 151, 154
Bon Jovi 216
Bon Jovi (Jon) 229
Bonamassa (Joe) 37, 80, 100, 111, 133, 215, 216, 217, 227, 228, 235
Bonham (John) 127
Boston 229
Bowen (John) 94
Bowie (David) 20, 150, 151, 153, 155, 190
Bradoka (Scott) 231
Brass Elephant 96
Brooks (Harvey) 109
Buckcherry 230
Buckethead 186
Buckingham (Lindsay) 5, 143
Bumblefoot 186
Burns 92
Butts (Ray) 70

C

Campbell (Mike) 171, 172
Canned Heat 145
Cantrell (Jerry) 195, 199, 201
Carter (Walter) 144
Cash (Johnny) 45
CBS 116, 161
Charvel 179, 190
Cheap Trick 105, 143, 145, 155, 188
Chess 42, 92
Chicago 125
Chicago Musical Instruments 33
Chicken Shack 231
Christian (Charlie) 15, 25, 146
Cinderella 183
Claesgens (Paul «Bleem») 96
Clapton (Eric) 19, 97, 99, 100, 101, 104, 105, 107, 108, 111, 114, 116, 127, 128, 135, 137, 142, 145, 156, 158, 186, 195
Clash (The) 151, 215
Cobain (Kurt) 199
Cochran (Eddie) 151
Colletti (Tommy) 230
Collins (Allen) 141
Coltrane (John) 108
Cooper (Alice) 185
Corea (Chick) 153
Cornell (Chris) 201
Cream 99, 100, 145
Creedence Clearwater Revival 21, 110, 120
Crosby (Bing) 16, 23, 25
Cunetto (Vince) 224
Curleigh (James «J.C.») 234, 235
Custom Shop 99, 100, 101, 105, 108, 118, 123, 132, 139, 146, 151, 157, 166, 167, 176, 180, 181, 186, 187, 188, 195, 199, 201, 209, 215, 217, 218, 222, 224, 227, 230, 235, 236

D

Dale (Dick) 82, 89
Dallas 92
Danelectro 82
D'Angelico 114
Dantzig (Joel) 101
DaPra (Vic) 229 , 231
Daughtry (Charles) 230, 231
Davies (Dave) 164
Davis (Miles) 153
DeCola (Jim) 234, 235
Deep Purple 136
DelRay (Dean) 209
Derek And The Dominos 137, 158
Derrig (Kris) 185
Derringer (Rick) 105
Deurloo (Jim) 180
Di Meola (Al) 21, 153, 155
DiMarzio 123
DiMarzio (Larry) 153
Dire Straits 175
Ditson 13
Dobro 13
Donegan (Lonnie) 92
Doors (The) 118
Dopyera (John) 13, 15
Dopyera (Rudy) 13, 15

Dowd (Tom) 88, 130, 137
Dylan (Bob) 108
Dzidzornu (Rocky) 119

E

Eagles 143, 155
Eddy (Duane) 82, 89
Egmond 92
Eko 92
Electric Flag (The) 108, 109
Ellington (Duke) 18
Epiphone 12, 15, 121, 133, 181, 185, 187, 193, 207, 210, 216, 217, 236
Erlewine (Dan) 108
ESP 186, 204, 207
Ezrin (Bob) 159

F

Farlow (Tal) 114
Felder (Don) 143
Fender 31, 33, 38, 58, 62, 67, 82, 108, 109, 114, 116, 141, 143, 144, 161, 175, 203, 224
Fender (Leo) 27, 29, 39, 132
Fitzgerald (Ella) 23
Fleetwood (Mick) 101, 143
Fleetwood Mac 5, 101, 111, 142, 155
Fogerty (John) 21, 118
Ford (Mary), Colleen Summers dite 23, 24, 25, 33, 37, 39, 41, 51, 58, 82, 88, 89
Foreigner 215
Frampton (Peter) 20, 100, 139, 215, 216
Framus 92
Franks (Melvyn) 103
Free 94, 109, 111, 136
Frehley (Ace) 20, 142, 181
Fripp (Robert) 118
Futurama 92

G

Garcia (Jerry) 124
Gatton (Danny) 216
Gelotte (Björn) 205, 207
Genesis 141, 155
Gibbons (Billy) 137, 138, 139, 157
Gibson 9, 10, 11, 12, 13, 15, 16, 23, 27, 28, 31, 33, 37, 38, 39, 41, 49, 51, 54, 55, 57, 58, 61, 62, 67, 69, 70, 72, 73, 75, 76, 82, 84, 85, 87, 88, 89, 100, 103, 105, 108, 113, 114, 116, 121, 122, 124, 125, 128, 132, 133, 135, 141, 143, 145, 146, 148, 153, 157, 161, 163, 164, 165, 166, 167, 175, 176, 179, 180, 181, 185, 186, 187, 195, 201, 203, 207, 212, 215, 216, 217, 218, 221, 222, 224, 229, 230, 233, 234, 235, 236
Gibson (Orville) 181
Gillis (Brad) 172
Gilmour (David) 124, 158
Glaser (Joe) 41
Goodman (Benny) 15
Gorham (Scott) 190
Gossard (Stone) 201
Gov't Mule 215
Grappelli (Stéphane) 18
Grateful Dead (The) 124
Gray (Johnny) 58
Green (Freddie) 13
Green (Peter) 101, 103, 104, 111, 141, 142, 157, 205, 209, 228
Green Day 215, 235
Gretsch 29, 51, 70, 82, 92, 94, 108, 116, 122, 141, 151, 161
Gretsch (Fred) 33
Gruhn (George) 231
Guitar Preservation 224

Guitar Slim 47
Guitar Trader 167
Guns N' Roses 132, 179, 183, 185, 186, 187, 188, 199, 201

H

Hackett (Steve) 141, 172
Hagar (Sammy) 142
Hagstrom 92
Haley (Bill) 67
Haley (Bill) and The Comets 58, 59
Hamer 101, 143
Hammett (Kirk) 103, 157, 204, 205, 209, 228
Hanna (Jeff) 230
Harmony 61
Harris (Norman) 169
Harris (Steve) 190
Harrison (George) 99, 105, 107
Heafy (Matt) 207
Heartbreakers (The) 148
Hendrix (Jimi) 99, 109, 118
Heritage Guitar Company (The) 180
Hetfield (James) 204, 205
Highbee (Cody) 235
Hinds (Brent) 201
Hiwatt 146
Hofner 92
Holland (W.B.) 45
Holly (Buddy) 92
Honeyman-Scott (James) 230
Hooker (John Lee) 42
Howe (Steve) 146
Humble Pie 135, 139, 155
Hunter (Steve) 185

I

Ibanez 169, 181, 203
Iggy And The Stooges 151
In Flames 205, 207, 235
Iommi (Tony) 234
Iron Maiden 190, 201, 216
Isbell (Jason) 144

J

Jackson 179, 185, 186, 190
Jackson (Michael) 169, 175
Jagger (Mick) 119
James Gang 127, 129, 143
Jeff Beck Group (The) 20, 104, 105
Jethro Tull 118, 146, 155
Jett (Joan) 212
Jimmy Wallace Guitars 167
John Mayall & The Bluesbreakers 97, 100, 101, 111
Johnny Thunders & The Heartbreakers 155
Johnson (Eric) 188
Jones (Adam) 199, 201
Jones (Brian) 94, 118
Jones (John Paul) 127
Jones (Mick) 151, 215
Jones (Steve) 151, 153, 171, 215
Journey 159, 172, 175
Juszkiewicz (Henry) 180, 181, 183, 229, 233, 234, 235

K

K&F 39
Kath (Terry) 125
Kauffman (Clayton «Doc») 39
Kay 203
Keifer (Tom) 183
Kelliher (Bill) 201
Kentucky Headhunters 230
Kessel (Barney) 114

K

King (Albert) 111
King (B. B.) 164, 216
King (Ed) 142, 144, 230
King (Freddie) 19, 42, 43, 47, 99
King Crimson 118, 128
King Records 42
Kinks (The) 95, 164
Kirwan (Danny) 101
Kiss 20, 142, 155
Knopfler (Mark) 175
Koehler (Mat) 233
Kooper (Al) 108
Korner (Alexis) 92
Kossoff (Paul) 94, 111
Krieger (Robby) 118

L

Landers (Paul) 205
Landreth (Sonny) 215
Larson (August) 13
Larson (Carl) 13
Leadbelly 92
Led Zeppelin 96, 126, 127, 128, 129, 132, 136, 157, 183
Lee (Alvin) 145
Lee (Jake E) 190
Lennon (John) 92, 105, 118, 146
Leo's 16
Les Paul and Mary Ford 23, 25, 89
Les Paul Trio 16, 25
Levy (John) 31
Lifeson (Alex) 215
Linhof (Kurt) 137
Little Richard 92
Loar (Lloyd) 28
Lover (Seth) 55, 67, 70
Lovin' Spoonful (The) 105, 108, 229
LTD 207
Lucas (Nick) 10, 11, 13, 18, 25, 33
Lukather (Steve) 169
Lynott (Phil) 190
Lynyrd Skynyrd 141, 144, 155, 230

M

McCartney (Paul) 216
McCarty (Ted) 27, 31, 41, 49, 51, 54, 55, 70, 114, 133
McCoys (The) 105
McCready (Mike) 201
McLaren (Malcolm) 151
McVie (Christine) 143
McVie (John) 101
Mahal (Taj) 118
Marsden (Bernie) 229
Marley (Bob) 146
Marriott (Steve) 135, 139
Marshall 99, 103, 111, 124, 127, 128, 136, 137, 141, 146, 151, 153, 168, 175, 186, 187, 193, 209, 218
Marshall (Jim) 99
Martin 13, 161, 175
Martin (George) 20
Martin (Greg) 230
Mastodon 201
Max Guitar 230
Mayall (John) 94, 97, 99, 101, 103, 104, 141
Melvins (The) 199, 201
Memphis 183
Metallica 103, 157, 204, 205, 207, 209, 235
Miles (Buddy) 109
Miller (Steve) 216
Miracles (The) 59, 67
Montrose 142, 155
Montrose (Ronnie) 142, 230
Moore (Gary) 103, 111, 157, 205, 209, 228
Moore (Scotty) 37, 82
Morrison (Van) 201
Motown 92
Mott The Hoople 146, 155, 231
Mountain 145, 146, 155
Murelli (Laurent) 80
Murphy (Tom) 224
Murphy Lab 227, 233

N

National 13
Nelson (Keith) 230
Ness (Mike) 21, 123
New Yardbirds (The) 127
New York Dolls 148, 151
Newton (Ernie) 16
Nicks (Stevie) 143, 230
Nielsen (Rick) 105, 143, 145
Night Ranger 172
Nirvana 199
Nitty Gritty Dirt Band 230
Niven (Alan) 185
Nono 212
Norlin 116, 180, 181

O

Okuda (Tamio) 230
Orville 181
Osborne (Buzz) 199
Osbourne (Ozzy) 190, 193, 201

P

Page (Jimmy) 9, 92, 95, 96, 97, 99, 100, 104, 114, 126, 127, 128, 129, 135, 157, 169, 181, 183, 186, 212, 215, 222
Pappalardi (Felix) 145
Paul (Les) Lester Polfuss dit 9, 10, 11, 12, 14, 15, 16, 17, 18, 23, 24, 25, 28, 31, 33, 37, 38, 39, 41, 51, 54, 58, 61, 62, 67, 69, 72, 82, 85, 88, 116, 124, 125, 130, 133, 141, 158, 159, 188, 203, 236
Paul Butterfield Blues Band (The) 108
Pearl Jam 201
Perkins (Carl) 45, 47
Perkins (Clayton) 45
Perkins (Jay) 45
Perry (Joe) 140, 142, 181, 183, 186, 188
Petty (Tom) 148, 171
Pike (Matt) 163, 164
Pink Floyd 124, 158
Plant (Robert) 127
Polfuss (George William) 10
Polfuss (Lester) see Paul (Les)
Polfuss (Ralph) 10
Pontillo (Jim) 76
Pop (Iggy) 151
Presley (Elvis) 37, 82, 89
Pretenders (The) 230
PRS 212
Pure Prairie League 20

Q

Quiet Riot 190
Quintette du Hot Club De France 18

R

Ralphs (Mick) 146, 231
Rammstein 205, 235
Raymond (Andrew) 231
Recording King 61
Reed (Lou) 185
Reed Smith (Paul) 212
Reeder (Mike) 230
Reinhardt (Django) 18, 25
Reiss (Andy) 115
Rendell (Stan) 114
Return To Forever 153
Rhoads (Randy) 190, 191, 193
Rhodes 143
Riboloff (J.T.) 181, 195
Richards (Keith) 19, 91, 94, 99, 104, 118, 119, 148, 183, 230
Rickenbacker 39, 42, 118, 127, 129, 141
Ritchie (Lionel) 169
Rizzo (Tom) 5
Robertson (Brian) 190
Robinson (Silvia) 58, 67
Robinson (Smokey) 59
Rolling Stones (The) 19, 94, 104, 105, 111, 118, 128, 148, 155
Ronson (Mick) 20, 105, 150, 151, 190
Rossington (Gary) 142
Rotten (Johnny) 153
Rumble Seat Music 218, 222
Rush 215, 216, 235

S

Sahlgren (Mark) 181
Santana 145, 155, 159
Santana (Carlos) 141, 143
Sax (Adolphe) 9
Scholz (Tom) 229
Schon (Neal) 159, 171, 172
Sebastian (John) 105, 108, 229
Selmer 94, 104, 111, 167
Sex Pistols 151, 153, 155
Shanks (John) 216, 229
Shaw (Tim) 161, 167, 181
Shirley (Kevin) 216
Silvertone 203
Simo (J.D.) 231
Sinatra (Frank) 58
Slash 179, 181, 183, 185, 186, 187, 188, 190, 193, 236
Slash's Snakepit 185, 186, 201
Sleep 163, 164
Slubowski (Mike) 229
Small Faces 139
Smeck (Roy) 33
Smith (Adrian) 190
Kessel (Barney) 114
Smith (Johnny) 114
Social Distortion 21, 123, 128
Soundgarden 199, 201
Spencer (Jeremy) 101
Spiders From Mars 20
Stanley (Paul) 142
Stills (Stephen) 108, 230
Stooges (The) 151, 155
Stradlin (Izzy) 183
Strings & Things 105, 167
Stutz (Evelyn) 10
Sumlin (Hubert) 42
Summers (Colleen) see Ford (Mary)
Sun 92
Supro 82
Sylvain Sylvain 148

T

Taplin (Marv) 59
Taylor (Mick) 19, 94, 104, 183
Ten Years After 145
Tharpe (Rosetta) 19, 42, 47, 88
Thayil (Kim) 199
The Edge 159, 171
Them 201
Thin Lizzy 103, 190, 193, 201
Thunders (Johnny) 148, 151
Timbrell (Hilmer « Tim ») 31
Tom Petty and The Heartbreakers 171, 172, 175
Tommy Dorsey & His Orchestra 231
Tool 199, 201
Toto 169, 175
Townshend (Pete) 92, 121, 123
Travers (Pat) 212
Travis (Merle) 28, 29, 31, 47
T-Rex 151, 153, 155
Trivium 207, 235

U

U2 159, 171, 175

V

Valley Arts 169
Van Halen 168, 175
Van Halen (Eddie) 168, 172, 190
Velvet Revolver 186
Velvet Underground 20
Ventures (The) 82, 89, 114
Vigier 186
Vincent (Gene) 92
Vox 127, 129

W

Wachtel (Waddy) 230
Walsh (Joe) 127, 129, 143, 157
Waring (Fred) 16
Waters (Muddy) 42, 92
Watkins 92
Watts (Charlie) 104, 119
Webb (Stan) 231
West (Leslie) 145, 146, 147, 148
West (Speedy) 28
Westgor (Nate) 96
Whiteman (Paul) 16
Whitesnake 229
Whitford (Brad) 142, 183, 188, 230
Who (The) 95, 123, 128, 136
Williamson (James) 151, 153
Wilson (Alan) 145
Wilson (Nancy) 58
Winter (Johnny) 145
Wittrock (Tom) 229
Wolf (Howlin') 42, 47
Wolverton (« Sunny » Joe) 16
Wong (Cory) 129
Wray (Link) 82, 89
Wurlitzer 143
Wylde (Zakk) 190, 192, 193, 204, 205, 215
Wyman (Bill) 119

Y

Yardbirds (The) 97, 99, 104, 127, 129
Yasgur (Max) 145
Yes 146, 155
Young (Angus) 111
Young (Neil) 105, 107

Z

Zappa (Frank) 105, 124
Zebrowski (Gary) 180
Zevon (Warren) 230
ZZ Top 132, 137, 138, 139, 157, 168

PICTURE CREDITS

THANKS TO:

Anna for proofreading and enduring my nonsense

Nicolas, Philippe, Emilie and Thomas (Olo), Zarko and Sara (ZS Studio), Chris, Mat, Marc, Romain, Mark, Jim, Cody and Libby (Gibson), Bumblefoot, Rick Beato, Eliot (Rumble Seat Music), Didier and Arnaud (Millésime Guitars), George (Gruhn Guitars), Walter (Carter Vintage Guitars), Pierre-Marie (Bass N Guitar), Big Dez, Andy Reiss, Julien (Hepcat), Laurent (Guitare Village), Susan (Guernsey's), Christophe Marain, NikoSlash, Steve Hackett